OVERCOMING OVERTHINKING

THE COMPLETE GUIDE TO CALM YOUR MIND BY
CONQUERING ANXIETY, SLEEPLESSNESS,
INDECISION, AND NEGATIVE THOUGHTS

KIRK TEACHOUT

CONTENTS

Introduction   7

1. BRAIN PAIN   15
   The Neuroscience of Overthinking   20
   Why Do We Do It?   24
   How Much Thinking is Too Much?   26
   What is Overthinking Doing to You and
   Your Life?   28
   Summary Box   34
   Segue   35

2. IT BEGINS WITH A THOUGHT   37
   Faulty Cognitive Biases   42
   How Do We Combat Cognitive Biases?   48
   Interactive Element   53
   Summary Box   53
   Segue   54

3. THE STRESS CYCLE   55
   Where Do Emotions Come From?   58
   What Are Emotions, Really?   62
   Emotional Needs   67
   Processing Unwanted Emotions   68
   Interactive Element   71
   Summary Box   72
   Segue   73

4. THINK ENOUGH, BUT NOT
   TOO MUCH   75
   How to Get Unstuck When You're Feeling
   Overwhelmed   79
   How Do You Know When You Have
   Enough Information to Make a Smart
   Decision?   83
   How to Make Good Decisions   84
   How to Be Agile and Responsive When
   Life Gets Tough   85
   How to Do a Basic Risk Assessment or
   Analysis   86
   Contingency Planning   88
   Fear-setting   88
   Interactive Element   89
   Summary Box   89
   Segue   90

5. END THE OVERWHELM   95
   What is Mental Overwhelm?   98
   Why Too Much Complexity Leads to
   Mental Breakdown   100
   What Are the Signs That a Breakdown is
   Imminent?   103
   How to Simplify Your Life   106
   Summary Box   108
   Segue   109

6. FAST CALM   111
   The Sympathetic Nervous System and the
   Parasympathetic Nervous System   114
   How Activating Your Parasympathetic
   Nervous System Can Lower Stress   116
   How to Engage Your Parasympathetic
   Nervous System   118
   Interactive Element   124
   Summary Box   125
   Segue   126

7. TRIGGERS   127
    What Triggers Your Overthinking?   130
    Root Causes of Overthinking Self-Quiz   140
    How Do I Recognize and Release My
    Overthinking Triggers?   141
    Understand How Your Core Beliefs Can
    Cause Overthinking   145
    How Do You Reframe and Shift
    Unhelpful Core Beliefs?   146
    Interactive Element   148
    Summary Box   150
    Segue   151

8. BREAKING THE HABIT   153
    How Are Thought Habits Formed?   156
    To Replace a Bad Habit, You Can Try
    These Steps   158
    Practicing Self-Compassion   163
    How Mindfulness Can Help You Master
    Your Mind, Body, and Life   165
    What Can Help You Be More Mindful?   167
    Interactive Element   170
    Summary Box   172

    Conclusion   173
    Resources   179

INTRODUCTION

> "You don't have to see the whole staircase, just take the first step."
>
> — MARTIN LUTHER KING, JR.

A few months after we had our second child, my wife, Lauren started looking for a new job. Unfortunately, everyone she interviewed with was looking to hire someone in the future. They were talking with possible prospects rather than hiring someone for an immediate position.

At the same time, I was watching our 1-year-old and our newborn while trying to run my business from home, but my business was not doing as well as it was before. During all of this, bills were coming in, our savings were dwindling, credit card debts were increasing, and I couldn't sleep. Lauren spent 7 weeks looking for an open position with nothing to show for it. This was when we went into panic mode. Throughout this process, we put our house up for sale, and the closing date was approaching the following week. Lauren and I were scrambling, trying to think, think, think — but we couldn't seem to grasp a solution. Between sleeplessness from raising a newborn, rising debt, and selling our house — with seemingly no end to the madness in sight — we were ready to give up.

Lauren had one final interview the week before our house was set to close, and it was 5 hours away. It seemed very promising, and we were hopeful. After meeting with the business again, the recruiter told Lauren that they were looking to possibly fill this position in the future. That long, silent, 5-hour drive home was defeating. It was depressing. It was one of the hardest times we have ever faced in our marriage.

This difficult time seeded thoughts of worry, anxiety, and the fear of not being good enough in my wife. She couldn't help but spiral into a cycle of overthinking. Were the positions with these companies truly not there yet, or was she not the right candidate for these jobs? Once these thoughts started to grow, they overflowed into other areas of our life. It put a strain on our marriage, and she started to question whether she was in the right industry to begin with.

"What if I'm stuck like this forever?" She would say, in her head, while lying in bed. "What if I'm incapable of being happy?" Little did she know, these nagging "what ifs" were one of the main things holding her back from achieving her goals and finding happiness in her life. Being a devoted husband to an overthinker got me overthinking a few things myself. Whenever we tried to have a conversation about her worries and anxiety, I felt paralyzed, not knowing how to answer. "How can I best support her?" I asked myself on several occasions. I received plenty of advice that should have been a solution — at least on paper. But nothing helped.

Lauren and I sloppily maneuvered our way through all of the situations life threw at us during that time, taking much-needed comfort in each other for the most part. Still, it was hard being 28, broke, and unhappy. Maybe you're experiencing something similar right now, and you should know that you're not alone. It's not easy treading water for weeks, months, or even years. It gets tiresome trying to keep your head above the surface.

Your mid to late twenties are a transitional period. You're not a kid anymore. Perhaps you're done with school and are just now entering the working world. In this day in age, it feels like it's almost impossible to find a career that matches your particular skill set. This can be awfully discouraging for a lot of people, and many in this age bracket end up overthinking everything. For people like us, the smallest inconvenience can feel like a total mess.

When the Covid-19 pandemic hit in 2020, a large number of people fell on hard times. As a result of the pandemic, our business was mandated to shut down with no end in sight. We could not pay our team, let alone our monthly bills. All we could do was sit around and wait. This was something a lot of people faced during this time. It was scary and discouraging not knowing when it was going to end.

Some even had to move back in with their parents due to financial hardship. Moving back in with your parents when you are in your mid-twenties or older can be somewhat of a shock to your system. It's scarily easy to fall into depression, and some might even try to self-medicate with drugs and alcohol. Living out of your old childhood bedroom can make you feel like you cannot properly grow as an adult and as a person. When young adults don't have room to grow and thrive, they'll often start to feel very dissatisfied with their lives.

Even for those whose parents didn't mind taking them under their roof when the pandemic hit, this was still an incredibly difficult time. You've undoubtedly noticed the impact the pandemic had on your own life, on society, and on the world. Things will never go back to the way they were before, which is both a good thing and a bad thing in limitless ways.

People who are prone to overthinking don't like change. We thrive on routine, and those of us who are new to the working world are not necessarily used to making ends meet — particularly in a world where work culture has gotten incredibly callous. The world has changed significantly since your parents were your age; chances are, they probably don't understand what you're going through.

As a society, there are parts of us that are broken, and that's sad — but we're also strong because of it. Like your muscles, when you engage in excessive exercise, you need time to heal. When you do heal, you're bound to be ten times stronger after the fact. It's hard to grow up and become an adult. It's complicated, heartbreaking, and lovely all at the same time. Life simultaneously feels endless and fleeting, and I'm not sure what to do about it other than just take it one day at a time.

Your young adult years tend to be full of change — which can be wonderful — but it can also be awfully jarring. Not only are you changing personally and professionally, but you're also seeing your friends and loved ones at different stages of achievement than you. Maybe your best friend got married at 27 while you're still single at 30. Maybe your sister started her own business at 29 while you're actively pursuing your ideal career at 31. Everyone seems to be a contender in this invisible race, against themselves and others — not to mention the various versions of how people present themselves on social media. Like my wife was, you may be unhappy at work. Perhaps you've experienced thoughts like: "what am I even doing with my life," or "what if I'm stuck in this same position forever?"

Do you see what I mean? Overthinking is a cyclical and dangerous cycle. It makes you feel stuck (a concept known as "analysis paralysis") because you're creating these endless possible scenarios in your head, but at the same time, you don't know what to do to make these scenarios happen (or not happen, if your anxiety makes everything feel like a catastrophe).

This state of paralysis and fear can make you feel like you're unable to be your authentic self. You may feel like you're losing sight of who you truly are, and close yourself off from your loved ones. You might also expe-rience a drop in energy because you're overexerting yourself by thinking too much. This can lead to loss of sleep and appetite, which means your physical and mental health could take a dive.

Does any of this sound familiar? If so, again, you're definitely not alone. I know this because I have been there. As has Lauren. We've been through our ups and downs, sometimes feeling like we couldn't pull ourselves out of this vicious cycle. Like so many others, we tried a lot of self-help books, but what really helped us was doing our own, detailed research.

We didn't focus on how to stop overthinking. We focused on identifying why we were overthinking. We spent months trying to find the root cause of our overthinking and researched practical solutions to help us overcome it. It often felt like we took two steps forward and one step back, but that was still one step further from where we were before.

Breaking away from a chronic tendency to overthink takes time. After much research and practical application, Lauren and I have put this book together to help others like us: regular people, living regular lives in a world that seems to be speeding by.

Instead of jumping into a series of cookie-cutter suggestions on how to stop overthinking, let's spend some time understanding you. Let's delve into how you may be overthinking and why. Then, let's take a look at the solutions you come up with, and find those that work for you in your own unique way.

As you read, you'll see reflection questions throughout this book. Try to take a moment and really think about each question. How do these questions apply to your experiences in life? Reflecting on these things is a necessary part of overcoming overthinking, so give it your best shot!

1

BRAIN PAIN

"Overthinking, also best known as creating problems that are never there."

— DAVID SIKHOSANA

When you're getting bombarded by an onslaught of disorganized, often self-deprecating thoughts, it can make it very difficult for you to focus on your work, get enough sleep, and generally live your life. You might find yourself wishing that your brain would just shut up for a few minutes. Those of us who are prone to overthinking certainly understand that sentiment!

Something Lauren and I learned while doing our research is that before you overcome your overthinking, you've got to *understand* your overthinking. So, what is overthinking, exactly? Is there really such a thing as thinking too much? To put it simply, people who are plagued by overthinking often cannot stop themselves from dwelling on the same thought over and over again. They might spend too much of their time and energy over-analyzing certain situations.

For example, an overthinker might worry that they've left the stove on while out at a social gathering. The stove becomes all they can think about for the rest of the evening, whereas someone who doesn't overthink everything wouldn't worry about it too much. An over-thinker might experience thoughts like: "what if the house catches on fire?" or "what if my pets get carbon monoxide poisoning?" Needless to say, these types of thoughts are more harmful than they are helpful.

It can be difficult to identify the difference between helpful and harmful thoughts. Most overthinkers have both, but they may be so intertwined with each other that it's hard to tell which thoughts are actually helpful among the onslaught of harmful thoughts. If you're worried you left your stove on, "what if my house catches on fire," is a harmful thought because the likelihood of that happening is incredibly small. A helpful thought, in this scenario, might be: "I always turn the stove off, so there's nothing to stress about." Dissecting these thoughts and differentiating between them can be quite helpful!

Reflection question: are the majority of my thoughts helping or harming me?

There are two types of overthinking, namely rumination and worrying. Rumination is cyclical and involves rehashing events that caused you pain or emotional turmoil in the past. Let's say you had a toxic friendship in high school, and this person made you feel like you were the problem. Even if you've grown up and realized they were the toxic one, you might still lie awake at night wondering what exactly you did wrong — even if you did absolutely nothing wrong!

Excessive worrying is slightly more common and typically involves hyper-focusing on something that's going to happen in the future. Maybe, for example, you've got a big presentation at work next week. You might start imagining every possible thing that could go wrong (i.e. "what if I get stage fright?" or "what if that one male coworker talks over me again?"). Someone who overthinks these things will have a hard time not feeling like a nervous wreck. Some might even panic and jump ship. They might think, "I can't do this," and avoid the responsibility altogether because they're stuck in a state of analysis paralysis.

Ruminating and obsessing over the things you can't control can cause what we call "brain pain." Basically, your brain gets so exhausted from overthinking that it gets stuck in that polarizing state of fear. You might find yourself breaking down more often than usual (i.e. getting overwhelmed by the smallest inconveniences). You might feel like your brain isn't functioning as it should because it's so overworked.

It's also important to keep in mind that overthinking is oftentimes a symptom of anxiety and depression. Anxiety and depression go hand-in-hand most of the time. Your overthinking tendencies may be a result of your anxiety, which then might trigger thoughts of worthlessness (depression). Attending weekly therapy and taking medication can sometimes help over-thinkers, but that's a bandaid, not a cure. Everyone is different, though, and it's definitely worth looking into — especially if you know you suffer from anxiety and/or depression.

Reflection question: How many signs of overthinking am I displaying in my life?

In order to gain a deeper understanding of your over-thinking tendencies, it can be helpful to know the signs. Everyone worries sometimes, but it can be diffi-cult to identify when your worrying has become a real problem. You should know that people who don't overthink things won't spend hours or even weeks stressing about a problem they have no control over. They're able to say: "well, there's nothing I can do about that right now," and simply go on with their lives.

This can be rather confusing for overthinkers. We can say mantras in our heads like "there's nothing I can do about that right now, and that's okay," or "this is not worth stressing about," but our brains won't stop nagging us. It can get to a point where the thoughts you're getting bombarded with are intrusive. You don't want to think these things; you just do!

So, the question becomes: how can I get rid of these thoughts? How can I prevent them from controlling my life? If you're going to reduce your overthinking tendencies, you're going to want to be able to identify the signs that indicate you're overthinking. For example, if you find yourself having a lot of negative thoughts or obsessing over things outside of your control, you're probably overthinking.

If you constantly feel anxious about something — and seem unable to think about anything else — that's a good indication that your overthinking has become a problem. You might feel mentally exhausted, or have a hard time relaxing even when nothing particularly stressful is happening in the moment. You might find yourself seeking reassurance from others, or being short or irritable with your loved ones.

Overthinkers always jump to the worst-case scenario, even if that scenario is not particularly logical. Think back to the example of worrying that you left your stove on and therefore your house might catch on fire. When you explain your thought process to someone, they might point out that the way you're thinking doesn't really make sense — which you'll know is true — but you won't be able to stop overthinking anyway. You'll second-guess yourself, and have trouble concentrating at work. You'll feel on edge and replay situations in your head, knowing full well that that type of thinking isn't productive.

THE NEUROSCIENCE OF OVERTHINKING

One of the best ways to understand overthinking is to understand the science behind it. Science rules, after all! Constant thinking is supposed to lead to problem-solving, but not all problems are easily solved just by thinking about them. When our problems are too complicated, we can get stuck in that paralyzing loop of overthinking. Although your energy is being drained from thinking too much, you're not making any progress, which can be incredibly discouraging.

Your brain is complicated, and like most issues that stem from mental illness, overthinking is largely chemical. You may not be aware of it, but when you engage in overthinking, the chemicals in your brain go into hyperdrive. These chemicals — namely dopamine, serotonin, adrenaline, and cortisol — react with one another in different and complex ways. This is where things get a bit complicated, so let's go over what each of these chemicals does in a bit more detail.

Dopamine

Dopamine plays a major role in your brain's functioning. If you've ever felt exceptionally happy after exercising or playing with your dog, for example, that's dopamine in action! Dopamine is very much connected to your brain's reward center. When you do something nice for yourself, dopamine gets released, and you feel a sense of satisfaction and pleasure.

A lot of people think of dopamine as "what makes you happy," but it also plays a role in regulating your emotions and driving your various motivations. People with proper dopamine levels might have an easier time focusing and staying motivated than those who are lacking dopamine. Overthinkers, for example, tend to lack dopamine, which can heavily contribute to that lethargic feeling you've probably grown accustomed to.

Serotonin

It's easy to confuse serotonin for dopamine. Both are happy emotion regulators, and upon release into your brain, serotonin and dopamine can make you feel like a million bucks. Serotonin, however, is much like a conductor. You have a symphony of neurotransmitters firing in your brain at all times, and serotonin is responsible for making sure things don't go haywire.

Serotonin plays a huge role in mood regulation, the way you compose yourself in certain situations, and your overall sense of well-being. If you feel calm and collected after going for a walk or drinking a nice cup of tea, for example, it's because these activities release serotonin. Having enough serotonin in your system is also crucial when it comes to maintaining a regular sleep schedule and a healthy appetite.

Adrenaline

People don't go bungy-jumping because it's pleasant and calming; they do it for the adrenaline rush. When you overcome a particular obstacle or do something you would never have dreamed of doing years ago, adrenaline gets released into your brain. Adrenaline is a very powerful thing. A mother whose infant has gotten trapped underneath a car, for example, will be able to lift the car up off of her child in order to save them — thanks to pure adrenaline!

Adrenaline also plays a role in properly regulating your blood pressure and heart rate. It's what helps you focus and overcome challenges that seem impossible. When the going gets tough, adrenaline is what gives you the energy and sometimes superhuman strength you need to accomplish anything. It can be an absolute godsend for overthinkers.

Cortisol

Cortisol is meant to be a guardian angel of sorts. It's responsible for regulating the way your body responds to stressful situations. When you're faced with something stressful or scary, cortisol gets released. This causes your blood vessels to constrict and your heart rate to increase, which prepares your body for whatever is about to happen next.

The problem with cortisol, though, is it can have negative effects on your brain and body if too much of it gets released. If you're constantly stressed, for example — like most overthinkers are — your body is going to get overloaded with cortisol. This is what causes symptoms like panic attacks, mood swings, and rumination. Not fun.

Reflection question: What might be at the root of my over-thinking?

WHY DO WE DO IT?

Asking "why do I overthink everything" might feel like you're overthinking your overthinking, but I promise — asking yourself this question is a necessary part of overcoming overthinking! People commonly overthink when attempting to solve their problems or make an important decision, not knowing that overthinking can actually cloud their judgment and negatively affect their decision-making process.

Overthinking can be habitual as well. A lot of people with severe overthinking tendencies have grown accustomed to using overthinking as a coping mechanism. It was the only way they knew how to deal with whatever challenging experiences they went through while growing up. Overthinking, then, can often be a trauma response. For example, if your mom had trouble finding work when you were a kid — and this heavily affected the well-being of your family — you might start overthinking every time a job interview doesn't pan out the way you wanted it to. This might be especially true if you're raising a family of your own! Generational trauma is very real, and as a young adult, you might have a tendency to not want to go through the same struggles your parents did.

At this point, you might be wondering: "well, I haven't experienced any significant trauma in my life, so why am I overthinking everything?" This is a good question, and to put it simply, excessive overthinking isn't always rooted in trauma. Many people develop overthinking tendencies later in life in response to a particularly stressful event. If you constantly feel stressed at work, this can also contribute to your overthinking habit. You might feel helpless at work or in other areas of your life, and overthinking can make you feel like you have some semblance of control.

A lot of overthinkers are perfectionists who fear failure — which is not in and of itself a bad thing — but if you can't reign it in a bit, you'll probably end up leading a pretty stressful life. Overthinking the problems in your life can feel like a good way to distract yourself from the possibility that you might fail. Overthinkers also tend to avoid conflict at all costs, which is mentally exhausting. Fear of conflict is again rooted in anxiety, so it's not something you want to ignore.

Furthermore, overthinking has some short-term, dopamine-boosting side effects that some people can subconsciously get addicted to. The people in their lives may express pity or sympathy for them, which, let's be honest, feels *good*. People also often overthink important decisions because they don't want to make these decisions in the first place, and I get that! It can feel like a lot of pressure.

It's also important to keep in mind that overthinking can be a symptom of OCD (Obsessive Compulsive Disorder). In fact, OCD is oftentimes the underlying cause of intrusive thoughts. If you truly feel like you can't stop your thoughts, and they're coming at you a million miles a minute, it might be a good idea to make an appointment with a psychiatrist.

HOW MUCH THINKING IS TOO MUCH?

Healthy thinking is all about balance, and admittedly, this balance can be hard to find. Thinking too much can make you feel like you're stuck in an endless loop, which is not going to help you solve your problems or make any crucial decisions. Thinking is complicated, and everyone has a different way of thinking. I don't really have a solid answer to the question: "how much thinking is too much" because that's something you need to figure out for yourself.

When you catch yourself overthinking, it's important to be mindful and try to take a step back. Think to yourself: "are these thoughts helpful or harmful?" Once you're able to identify the line between useful thinking and overthinking, you'll have a much easier time making sense of the issues you're facing in your life.

I will say that if your thinking is taking over every aspect of your life, you're probably thinking too much. If your overthinking leaves you feeling too paralyzed to do things like go to the grocery store or take care of yourself, then that's definitely an issue that needs to be addressed. If worrying about one thing leads to worrying about a number of other things, that's also an indication that you're thinking too much.

For example, if you're worried about whether or not you can afford to get takeout, you might then start worrying if you'll be able to afford rent that month. This might, in turn, lead to worrying about your job (i.e. "what will I do if I lose my job?"), which might make you start thinking about your career as a whole and whether or not your current career is even right for you.

As you can see, it's a vicious cycle. Most people don't even realize they're overthinking when they're doing it. It's hard to notice yourself overthinking when you're so caught up in, well… your thoughts. Thankfully, the more you learn to harness your overthinking, the more you'll be able to effectively reduce it!

WHAT IS OVERTHINKING DOING TO YOU AND YOUR LIFE?

If you're an overthinker, it's time to reassess (but not overthink!) your life. By identifying the ways in which overthinking has impacted your life, you'll be able to start doing the work necessary to overcome it. Many people don't know this, but overthinking has physical effects as well as emotional effects. You can use the checklist below to evaluate your overthinking and get a better grasp on what you've been going through.

Keep in mind that you don't need to check off "severe" for every category listed below to be considered an overthinker. Some of the categories on this list might surprise you because it's not commonly known that symptoms like overeating skin disorders can be caused by overthinking. It makes sense the more you think about it, though. These symptoms (and many others on this list) are rooted in anxiety — which is a big reason people overthink.

Rate yourself as "mild," "average," or "severe" for each category listed below:

Lack of focus:

- Mild
- Average
- Severe

Irritability:

- Mild
- Average
- Severe

Stress:

- Mild
- Average
- Severe

Anxiety:

- Mild
- Average
- Severe

Insomnia:

- Mild
- Average
- Severe

Undereating:

- Mild
- Average
- Severe

Overeating:

- Mild
- Average
- Severe

Racing thoughts:

- Mild
- Average
- Severe

Gut pain and/or digestive issues:

- Mild
- Average
- Severe

Hyperreactivity:

- Mild
- Average
- Severe

Indecision:

- Mild
- Average
- Severe

Procrastination:

- Mild
- Average
- Severe

Analysis paralysis:

- Mild
- Average
- Severe

Brain fog:

- Mild
- Average
- Severe

High blood pressure/chest pain/tachycardia:

- Mild
- Average
- Severe

Skin disorders — eczema, psoriasis, etc:

- Mild
- Average
- Severe

Increased heart rate:

- Mild
- Average
- Severe

Dizziness:

- Mild
- Average
- Severe

Headaches:

- Mild
- Average
- Severe

Nausea:

- Mild
- Average
- Severe

Fatigue:

- Mild
- Average
- Severe

Depression:

- Mild
- Average
- Severe

SUMMARY BOX

Overcoming overthinking won't be easy, but with the right tools on hand, it's absolutely possible. Remember: understanding your overthinking tendencies is a huge part of coping with and eventually overcoming them. Try talking to a therapist or journaling about where you think your overthinking stems from. By addressing the root cause of your overthinking habit, you'll be able to better understand and overcome it. Keep in mind, through it all, that overthinking affects millions of people all over the world. You're not alone, and you will get through this!

SEGUE

Reducing your overthinking starts with analyzing what is actually going on inside your head. Learning to question those "what ifs" that seem a little bit outlandish can help you gain a better understanding of which thoughts are helpful and which thoughts are harmful. Working with your thoughts and analyzing them in a healthy way might sound like mental gymnastics, but it's all part of overcoming overthinking. See for yourself!

2

IT BEGINS WITH A THOUGHT

> *"Worrying is like a rocking chair. It gives you something to do, but it doesn't get you anywhere."*
>
> — VAN WILDER

Thoughts are like a solar system. A vast expanse of never-ending stars. Some peter out over time and fade into nothingness. Some shine brighter than all the others and form constellations against the night sky — a network of thoughts, so to speak. Like stars, our thoughts are what guide us home when the world seems all too dark. What are we supposed to do, though, when our thoughts guide us in the wrong direction?

One of the most important things I've come to learn is that you are what you think, and perhaps even more so, you are what you do. Your thoughts are informed by your experiences — the good and the bad. They've formed into what they are today because of what you've been told by your parents, or taught by your teachers in school. As you get older, you learn how to think for yourself, and that becomes the foundation for who you are as a person.

Let's say, for example, that your parents told you all about their political views when you were a kid. Or, maybe, you just overheard them talking about it. It's natural for kids to mirror their parents, and that includes what they say, do, and think. Perhaps you went to school and talked at length about things you knew nothing about, simply because that's what you heard the adults around you conversing about.

Maybe someone told you that you were wrong — that the way you were thinking was *wrong* — and that made you feel bad inside. How, after all, could your parents be wrong? Perhaps you felt defensive at first, but later came to realize that your parents' way of thinking didn't actually sit right with you. Around the age of 12, your thinking gets more complex, which is why some people stop relying on the information their parents give them when they reach adolescence.

When you were in high school or college, you may have started doing your own research and forming your own thoughts about things. You may have also started experiencing intrusive or unwanted thoughts around this age, which undoubtedly made things a bit more complicated. When you're in your twenties and thirties, it becomes your responsibility to figure out which thoughts are truly your own and which thoughts are doing more harm than good.

Taking your thoughts by the reigns isn't easy, but practice makes perfect. Being mindful and open to even the bad thoughts — letting them pass over you like water off a duck's back — is the key to being stoic and overcoming overthinking. A big part of being a mindful thinker and practicing stoicism is asking yourself where your thoughts are coming from in the first place.

Reflection question: Where do my thoughts come from?

The truth is, your thoughts determine your reality. They affect everything that you are and that you're going to be — your emotions, your choices, your actions, and even your physical state of being. This is why people with overthinking tendencies often feel like they're drowning. Their thoughts are often all over the place, misinformed, or fueled by mental illnesses like anxiety, depression, and OCD. Usually, if your thoughts are faulty or unclear, your actions will be misguided.

Thankfully, though, there are a few ways you can combat this. You see, your thoughts don't actually hold any real power over you. They're just thoughts! You don't have to ignore your bad thoughts, necessarily, but you also don't have to feed the fire. For example, let's say you're having a particularly bad day and your brain is telling you things like "you're worthless," or "you'll never amount to anything." If you engage with these thoughts, you're simply entertaining the mean voice in your head.

If you continue to engage with your harmful thoughts, it can significantly affect your well-being. Not only will you start to believe that these thoughts are true, but you'll also begin to feel bad physically. You might feel sick to your stomach, or emotionally fatigued. You might feel like you want to crawl into bed and not speak to anyone for the rest of the night. This is what I call "curling up to your depression." Wallowing in your negative thoughts might seem warm and inviting, but it's actually a weight on your chest that keeps you from living your life to the fullest.

At this point, maybe you're thinking something along the lines of: "yes, I know they're just thoughts, but thoughts are pretty powerful and I can't help feeling down on myself." This is very real, and I'm not here to tell you how to feel. Sometimes you really can't help what you feel. You can, however, help what you think if you're willing to put the necessary work in. Trust me. It's worth it.

One thing you can do to combat your negative thoughts is instead try to engage with your positive, self-empowering thoughts. Your negative thoughts might seem a lot louder than your positive thoughts, but it's sort of like that one guy who used to steal your lunch money and belittle you back in high school: he's just a bully, and you don't have to listen to him.

When your thoughts of worry and worthlessness are bringing you down, you've got to dig deep and consider all of the amazing parts of yourself. Yes, you had a bad day, but you did a really great job standing up for yourself at work and you should be proud of yourself for that. Yes, you fumbled a few orders at the restaurant you work at, but now that you're home, you can focus your time and energy on doing something you love.

When you get trapped in the cycle of overthinking, it's important to consider which thoughts are actually real. Remember, the human brain is incredibly complicated. Your synapses are firing all the time, and your actions are releasing chemicals that react with one another in strange ways. It's easy to feel like your thoughts are surrounding you from all sides, but you don't need to let them dogpile you. You're stronger than that.

Reflection question: Are my thoughts always real or true?

FAULTY COGNITIVE BIASES

So, why in the world do we experience thoughts that aren't true? Why do we let these thoughts negatively impact us, even when we *know* they're not true? The answer is quite fascinating and surprisingly simple. All of us, in our everyday lives, are heavily under the influence of cognitive biases. Cognitive biases distort your thinking and influence your beliefs, so much so that many believe their cognitive biases to be the absolute truth.

In order to better understand how cognitive biases work — and how these biases affect your thinking — let's go over some of the most common types of cognitive biases people face in their daily lives below:

The Confirmation Bias

It's undeniably human to want to be validated in your beliefs. Most people develop a confirmation bias because they only listen to or seek out information that confirms their own beliefs. Let's say, for example, that your uncle believes the earth is flat. Despite there being way more sources available that prove the earth is spherical, he's going to seek out the one or two sources

OVERCOMING OVERTHINKING | 43

that "prove" the earth is flat — simply because he has a confirmation bias.

People with a strong confirmation bias oftentimes won't be able to think logically about what they've already decided is true. If an overthinker truly believes they're worthless, they won't believe you when you tell them they're not. Some overthinkers might even participate in what is known as "digital self-harm," which involves going on chat forums and asking strangers to validate their thoughts and feelings of worthlessness.

The Anchoring Bias

It's also human nature to believe that the first thing you think is what is truly "correct." No one likes admitting they're wrong, therefore, people who have a difficult time swallowing their pride might end up developing an anchoring bias. For example, a doctor who misdiagnoses a patient the first time they see them might refuse to consider other diagnoses when the same patient inevitably comes in again. It's an "I'm right, and that's final," kind of mindset.

People with overthinking tendencies may develop this particular bias when it comes to things like job searching. If they already have an idea in their head of what they want their career path to be, they might be unwilling to branch out and try something that would ultimately end up working better for them. They have already latched onto this "ideal career," and no other career can compare in their mind because they're influenced by a heavy anchoring bias.

The Hindsight Bias

Have you ever had a conversation with a friend where you admitted something to them, and they said something along the lines of: "Ha! I knew it all along!" We love being able to "predict" things, don't we? The hindsight bias is what gets people into things like betting and gambling, despite the fact these things don't always work out in the gambler's favor.

The hindsight bias is a pretty common one, and it's particularly strong because logic can occasionally be used to back up some hindsight biases. The hindsight bias often goes hand-in-hand with the confirmation bias as well. Your uncle, who believes the world is flat, might be absolutely convinced that a certain political candidate is going to win an election because of the "evidence" they've seen online.

The Misinformation Effect

Memory is a funny thing. Even if a particular memory seems crystal clear in your mind, it might not be entirely reliable or true to what actually happened. Research on the subject shows that memory is incredibly susceptible. Watching news coverage of an event you personally witnessed can skew your memory of what actually happened, for example. This, of course, would also skew your thought process regarding that particular event.

As much as we like to believe we can remember things perfectly well, most people's memories are flawed and full of gaps. This is totally normal, but it can, unfortunately, lead to people experiencing false beliefs and spreading misinformation based on those beliefs. Your brain doesn't particularly like memory gaps, so it will often fill them in with what it believes to be true.

The False Consensus Effect

We like to believe that our friends and family members will always agree with us on everything no matter what. You can of course still love someone without fully agreeing with them on certain things, but it's always nice when people agree with you, don't you think? The false consensus effect occurs when people automatically believe that the people around them have the same values as they do.

According to research, this effect stems from people spending too much time with people who *do* have the same exact values as them — so much so that they start to believe the majority of the world's population thinks the same way they do. This bias can significantly impact your thinking, as you might not be able to see or understand things from other perspectives.

The Halo Effect

First impressions are everything, but they aren't always correct. The halo effect is the tendency for people to have preconceived notions about a person based on their physical appearance. This is where the concept of "pretty privilege" comes from. Studies have shown that people are far more likely to believe and follow the ideas of someone who society considers physically attractive.

This cognitive bias can be particularly powerful. As unfair as it is, people who are perceived as more attractive are more likely to land jobs than those who are perceived as "average" or "unattractive." For people who overthink everything, not acing a job interview can lead them to believe that they're "too ugly" for that particular job. In reality, things aren't that black and white, but the halo effect does play a prominent role.

The Self-Serving Bias

It's wonderful to succeed, but it's also okay to fail sometimes. Nobody's perfect, and a lot of overthinkers have a hard time accepting this. The self-service bias is essentially the tendency for people to praise themselves for their successes but blame their failures on things outside of their control. For example, when you do well on an exam at school, you'll be proud of yourself for working hard (as you should be.) If you don't do well on the exam, you might feel a bit disappointed in yourself, whereas someone with a self-serving bias will say: "I failed because other students were being too loud," or "I failed because the teacher didn't prepare us well enough."

The Optimism Bias

There are certainly some people who are more pessimistic than optimistic, but most of us are honestly too optimistic for our own good. People with an optimism bias tend to believe that there's no way a negative life event — like divorce, for example — could possibly happen to them, despite the fact that divorce rates are constantly rising. Overthinkers with an optimism bias might go into a job interview so sure that they're going to get the job only to find out that the recruiter has already offered the job to someone else.

In this way, optimism can be dangerous. It can be difficult to find a healthy balance between optimism and pessimism, but it's a good idea to try to do so in order to save yourself some heartbreak and disappointment. Sometimes good things happen, and sometimes bad things happen. It's all just part of life. As you get older, though, things will get better. It's not too optimistic to think that!

HOW DO WE COMBAT COGNITIVE BIASES?

Because cognitive biases are often something we experience subconsciously, it can be tricky to identify and appropriately address them. There are quite a few strategies you can use to reduce the extent to which your cognitive biases are affecting you, however. One thing that can help is being open to multiple perspectives from people with different backgrounds and experiences than your own. The world is vast, and there's more than one way to look at, well, everything! You might even discover something new about yourself.

It can also be helpful to be aware of some of the more common biases, such as the confirmation bias and the hindsight bias. If you catch yourself reacting to certain situations based on your biases, you'll be able to put a stop to them and think about the situation at hand with some clarity. This is a big part of practicing mindfulness as well. When you suspect your reacting to something based on a cognitive bias, take a step back and consider what might be influencing you to think in a certain way.

Another way people combat their cognitive biases is by taking lots of time to reflect. Consider journaling about your thoughts in order to make more sense of them, and again, remember to take other perspectives into account. It's also a good idea to try to seek out disconfirming evidence of what you believe is true. This will help you gain more knowledge of the subject, as well as not feed your confirmation bias.

It's also recommended that you practice your critical thinking skills. This involves questioning the validity of the evidence you would normally perceive as good enough "proof" of your opinions being "correct," and breaking down your own preconceived assumptions and judgments in order to make more accurate decisions about things. You should also try to keep in mind that challenging your cognitive biases takes time! It's not easy to always be aware of your own thoughts and biases, but the more you put the effort in, the more you'll notice a difference.

Examining Your Thoughts

Most people don't know how much you can improve your life just by taking the time and space to examine your own thoughts. If you're familiar with Cognitive Behavioral Therapy, you've probably heard the phrase "inner critic" before. Everyone has a negative inner critic — a voice that basically amplifies your deepest insecurities. "You're worthless," the inner critic might say. "You're a hack. There's no way you'll get that job." Remember what I said earlier about the high school bully? *That's* your inner critic.

Observing your thoughts with mindfulness takes time and practice. We often think in negative patterns, which is how we get stuck in these seemingly endless cycles of overthinking. By identifying your negative thinking patterns and learning how to shift your unhelpful thoughts to the side (to make more room for your helpful ones!), you can dig yourself out of this vicious cycle.

Reflection question: Can I control my thoughts?

Mastering Your Focus

A lot of people with overthinking tendencies don't know where to focus their attention. Your brain is saying, "hey, what if you don't ace that job interview?" and "hey, what if you can't afford rent this month," and "hey, hey, hey —" Needless to say, it can be pretty relentless! If you're anything like Lauren and me, your negative thoughts have probably distracted you from completing various important tasks, like putting dinner on the table, or (if you're a student) getting your schoolwork done.

Thankfully, there are several helpful strategies you can use to strengthen your focus and improve your ability to concentrate on what's most important. For example, breaking your work down into smaller, more manageable chunks and prioritizing your tasks based on urgency can help you complete your work without getting overwhelmed by the amount of work you have to do.

It's also a good idea to eliminate distractions as much as you can. It's going to be pretty difficult to focus on the task at hand if you're attempting to scroll through Twitter and watch Youtube videos at the same time. I also recommend getting yourself a pair of noise-canceling headphones, as this can help a lot when it comes to reducing noisy distractions!

If you're working on something that you know is going to take a particularly long time, you can try out the Pomodoro Technique. This technique is super cool, and it honestly works wonders. The Pomodoro technique involves working on a task for about 25 minutes, then taking a short break so that you don't get burnt out. After four "pomodoros," you get to take an even longer break. Think of it as rewarding yourself with a break for getting 25 minutes of work done!

Naturally, it's also important to practice mindfulness throughout each day. Mindfulness techniques — like focusing on your breathing when you're feeling anxious or practicing mindful meditation — can be more helpful than you might think. Practicing mindfulness takes a lot of practice and time though, so don't feel frustrated if it doesn't help right away.

Finally, you should always take regular breaks during your work day. Moving your body is good for your brain, so taking a break to walk around or stretch every now and then is definitely a good idea. Going for a short walk or simply getting up from your chair for a few minutes is also a great way to clear your head if you feel yourself entering into a cycle of overthinking.

INTERACTIVE ELEMENT

Recording and monitoring your thoughts is a big part of Cognitive Behavioral Therapy. When you experience a thought, try to write down how you reacted emotionally and practically after the fact. This is a great way to learn how to control and understand your thoughts, which is a crucial part of eventually overcoming your overthinking tendencies.

SUMMARY BOX

Understanding and harnessing your thoughts takes a lot of time and practice, but it's certainly possible — especially when you have the right information and tools on hand. It's important to be mindful of your own cognitive biases, as these can severely skew your thinking. One way to be more aware of your cognitive biases is by taking the time to reflect on them. This might mean journaling or talking with a therapist about the biases you already know you have. Examining your thoughts every now and then by practicing mindfulness and removing distractions from your workspace is also a great way to combat cognitive biases and tighten the reigns on your thinking.

SEGUE

What goes hand-in-hand with thoughts? Emotions, of course! Your thoughts are oftentimes what cause you to feel emotions like joy, sorrow, excitement, and anger. Those with overthinking tendencies often have a difficult time regulating their emotions, but don't worry! We'll talk about that next.

3

THE STRESS CYCLE

> *"Simple can be harder than complex: You have to work hard to get your thinking clean to make it simple. But it's worth it in the end because once you get there, you can move mountains."*
>
> — STEVE JOBS

One of the most important things I've learned during this process is it can be difficult to separate your thoughts from your emotions. Both are complicated, and can seem nonsensical at times. Both invoke feelings in you that you might not necessarily know how to cope with. The fact of the matter is, there's quite a lot of overlap between thoughts and emotions. They're intertwined — often grotesquely fused together — and it's your job to pull them apart.

This is, of course, easier said than done. Your thoughts create your emotions, and your emotions create your thoughts. The problem is, your emotions can sometimes keep you from thinking rationally. If you're prone to overthinking, you're probably well aware of this! For a lot of us who overthink things, our thoughts are purely fear-based — meaning we cannot shake our thoughts free of fear. This typically ends up creating a stress response in your mind and body, and greatly contributes to the cycle of overthinking. Thankfully, though, breaking this cycle is totally possible. It's just a matter of being more mindful and learning how to regulate your emotions.

It can be challenging to wrap your head around the way your thoughts and emotions work, so I'll compare your thoughts to a forest fire that's fueled by your emotions — just to make things a bit more tangible. A thought could be like a spot of sunlight, shining through the treetops onto the dry brush at a very particular angle. This wouldn't necessarily start a fire right away, but let's say the dry brush is being blown about by the wind and air is exceptionally hot that day.

Let's say you've been going through a rough patch in a relationship. Once you've cooled down after having an argument, you might have a thought like: "I shouldn't have said that to my partner." This is sure to bring out some emotions — sadness, regret, anger, self-pity — which will undoubtedly spark more thoughts. "They're going to hate me, now. They're going to break up with me." These thoughts are going to spark more negative emotions, and so on and so forth.

Do you see how this cycle is like a forest fire? If you can't get your thoughts and emotions under control, they're going to keep spreading. They're going to destroy everything in their wake — *unless* you equip yourself with the tools needed to effectively fight them. What I'm trying to say is, all of us have the power to be metaphorical fire fighters. Mindfulness is a fire extinguisher, and self-care is the baking soda you sprinkle on top of the ashes.

Try to keep in mind that fighting your thoughts should be a **relaxed process**. You're not "fighting" them the same way you would fight an illness or a war. You're simply letting them wash over you. You're letting your thoughts and feelings happen, but you're not letting them control you. This takes practice, of course, but it can be immensely helpful in terms of relieving your stress.

Reflection question: Where do my feelings come from?

Gaining an understanding of where your feelings are coming from in the first place is a crucial step in eventually overcoming the thoughts that tend to send you into that vicious cycle of overthinking. When you experience a troubling thought, you can ask yourself: "okay, so where is this thought coming from?" Once you figure that out, you can say: "this is why I'm having this thought, but I don't have to let it build and grow."

People with overthinking tendencies often have the mindset that they *can't* control their thoughts. You might feel like you can't help overthinking about everything; that your thoughts just sort of happen and they're nothing you can do to stop them. I've been there too, so I get it! Your thoughts can make you feel like you're drowning. The thing is, you don't have to try to stop your thoughts from happening. They're going to happen no matter what. It's just a matter of learning how to swim against the current.

WHERE DO EMOTIONS COME FROM?

Emotions can come from pretty much anywhere, but most of the time, they're born from a mixture of multiple different factors. Experts still have a lot to learn about how emotions work, as well as what we can do to properly regulate them. It's also worth mentioning that some people will have an easier time regulating their emotions than others. Emotional dysregulation is typically a trauma response. Those who suffer from disorders like PTSD and ADHD may especially struggle. Let's go over some of the main factors that may be triggering your emotional responses below:

Physical State

Did you know that your physical state (i.e. the way your body feels) is heavily linked to your emotional state? When you're hungry or tired, for example, you might feel irritable or sad. At the same time, when you feel sad, your body might feel lethargic or achy. Your physical and emotional states are deeply intertwined, which is why it's so important to take care of your body as well as your mind.

You can even alter your emotional state by changing your posture. For example, if you slouch during a job interview, you're probably going to feel defeated. You might think to yourself: "I'm not going to get this job, so why even try in the first place?" If you sit up straight and make eye contact during your interview, however, you're probably going to feel a whole lot more confident — and this will show through to your potential employer.

Your physical state can also have an impact on the amount of neurotransmitters (like dopamine and serotonin) in your brain. If you've been to a doctor or therapist recently, they have recommended implementing a daily exercise regime into your routine. This is because physical exercise releases all of those feel-good neurotransmitters and hormones — dopamine, serotonin, endorphins, you name it — which in turn can reduce your stress and make you feel happier in general.

Chemical Imbalances

The brain is awfully complicated, which means chemical imbalances are awfully common. Your various chemical imbalances could be contributing to your emotions more than you realize they are. Big emotions like sadness, anxiety, joy, and love are associated with specific neurotransmitters, so if these neurotransmitters are imbalanced, it can cause your emotions to go somewhat haywire.

If your serotonin levels are low, for example, you might feel more depressed or anxious than usual. Similarly, if you have a dopamine imbalance, you might not feel motivated to do the things you usually love doing. These feelings can often snowball into other feelings, which often sparks the overthinking cycle. You might think: "why am I feeling this way?" You might wonder why you can't bring yourself to paint, write, draw, or exercise. "These things are what make me happy, and I know that," you'll tell yourself as you lie awake at night. "So, why don't I want to do them?"

There are plenty of reasons why people experience chemical imbalances, the most common of which is genetics. Things like your diet, certain medications, and your environment can have a significant impact, too. Talking with a therapist and taking antidepressants or anti-anxiety medications can sometimes help those who suffer from chemical imbalances. Exercising every day can also help you regulate your emotions better, as can practicing mindfulness when your stressors get activated.

Life Events

As human beings, a lot can happen to us throughout our lives. When you're a kid, you go through events like learning to ride a bike and losing your first tooth. Some kids may experience especially stressful events, like their parents getting divorced or their pets passing away. As you get older, you typically experience events like falling in love for the first time, getting your first job, and dealing with things like deaths in the family and financial difficulties.

Life events like this are *a lot* to cope with, especially for overthinkers. You might feel euphoric after your wedding and feel stressed out a week later because you realize you have to move and get a new job. You may also experience different strong emotions at different times about the same event. If you've ever gone through a rough breakup, for example, you might have felt relieved at first. Weeks after the breakup, however, you may have started missing your ex — despite the fact that the relationship was toxic. Brains are strange, and emotions often flip-flop! This is why it's so hard for overthinkers to regulate their emotions.

WHAT ARE EMOTIONS, REALLY?

Emotions can be scary and overwhelming, which is why it's common practice for people to avoid them. Understanding what emotions are and where they come from can help you learn to engage with them properly. This is not something most of us are taught growing up, the reason being that older adults (like your parents) oftentimes have trouble addressing and regulating their emotions as well.

Emotions are complicated, and it can be difficult to pinpoint which emotion or emotions you're feeling at any given time. Research suggests that there are ten primary emotions, namely fear, happiness, disgust, sadness, trust, distrust, shame, contempt, satisfaction, and amusement. There are then the emotions that branch off of these emotions (i.e. anger branches off of distrust and grief branches off of sadness). You can keep your emotions somewhat organized by thinking of them as an "emotional tree" of sorts.

Most of us have been taught to embrace our positive emotions and avoid our negative emotions, but this tendency to avoid can actually end up leading to an influx of emotional problems. You've probably heard that you shouldn't bottle up your bad feelings, as this only allows them to build up. This is basically the same principle. It's okay to feel that anger, shame, and fear — but don't let these emotions control you.

Come to think of it, you shouldn't let your positive emotions influence you too much either. Negative emotions can also masquerade as positive emotions, which is definitely something to be aware of. Let's say, for example, you quit your job because you were unhappy in that particular position. You might feel a boost of happiness and energy and go out drinking with your buddies to celebrate.

You might realize part way through the night, however, that you don't know what you're going to do now. You might start to feel some sadness and regret over quitting your job, especially if you needed that job to be able to pay your bills. Alcohol use can also force you to feel your negative emotions, but not in a particularly healthy way. Drinking because your sad is only going to make you feel more sad, so even if it works as a temporarily stress-reliever, I wouldn't recommend it.

Emotions, as you'll come to learn, are the messengers that inform you about your mental state. It's like when you scrape your knee and your pain receptors send a message to your brain that says: *"hey, you scraped your knee and it hurts!"* When you go through emotional pain, or "brain pain," your receptors react in a similar way. This happens because your brain is trying to protect you. It's saying: *"hey, the way you're feeling right now is emotionally painful!"*

Again, it's *a lot* to cope with. It really is. If your physical and emotional states are unbalanced, it can make things even more complicated. Your emotions can cause you to have misleading thoughts, which can lead you back to the cycle of overthinking you've become so familiar with. What can be done about this? Well, I'll get into that next.

Reflection question: is it possible to feel consistently different (better) than how I do now?

Learning how to properly regulate your emotions may seem insurmountable, and granted, it's hard work. Just the sheer thought of it makes a lot of people — especially overthinkers — freeze in their tracks. You're essentially training yourself to become a mindful thinker rather than an overthinker. Keep in mind that this takes practice, so if you do find yourself falling back into your overthinking habits even while trying to be mindful, don't be too hard on yourself about it. That's a part of being mindful, too!

So, how exactly should you go about regulating your emotions better? There's no cookie-cutter answer, and every person is different, but studies have shown that it can help to curate your thoughts. This involves learning how to properly focus your attention on the tidbits of actual useful information buried within your thoughts. It's sort of like digging for treasure. Every now and then, you'll strike gold! You just have to be mindful of the fact that sometimes you'll strike fools gold instead.

Learning how to curate your thoughts is all about being mindful of the things you think about, and how you think about them. Once you start to successfully curate your thoughts, you should find that you're able to think a lot more clearly as well as express yourself to others in a more effective way. This can be especially helpful for those with overthinking tendencies, as we tend to have a hard time expressing ourselves (what with all the thoughts bouncing around in our heads).

To curate your thoughts essentially means to think with intention. It means examining your mental and emotional state, and picking and choosing what you're going to focus on at any given moment. Scanning your mind and body is a big part of mindful meditation as well. It can help you feel grounded and in control, which should in turn help you gain control of your thoughts.

If you're going to get better at regulating your emotions, you're also going to want to start practicing self-care. You'd be surprised how much difference taking care of your body can make when it comes to your mental health. Staying hydrated, eating a proper diet, getting enough sleep, and exercising daily will — without question — make you feel better. Self-care takes work, though, and it can be difficult to establish a routine for yourself at first.

A lot of people who have trouble organizing their thoughts tend to have trouble staying organized in general. It makes sense. If you're unable to keep things straight in your head, it's not going to be very easy to keep things from going topsy-turvy in most areas of your life. Some find it helpful to keep a bullet journal, which can be an especially enjoyable way to organize your thoughts. Some come up with a meal plan and carry a water bottle around with them so that they don't fall behind on hydrating.

Finding a self-care routine that works for you can take some time, and the process is often one of trial and error. Keep in mind that it can take time for your body to adjust to a new routine. Mindful meditation, for example, can feel a bit silly at first — but you've got to stick with it. It won't do you any good to meditate for two minutes and then decide that it doesn't work for you. You haven't even given yourself a chance!

EMOTIONAL NEEDS

Everyone has emotional needs. A common reason people may feel frustrated or dissatisfied with their lives is because these emotional needs aren't being met in one way or another. You've probably noticed how good it feels to be appreciated, to accomplish something, or to be accepted as part of a community. These things are quite emotionally nourishing to us! We drink them in like water, and thrive.

If you're feeling badly about something — or over-thinking about a certain situation — chances are, your emotional needs aren't being met. Everyone deserves to be loved and cherished; to feel safe, and to go through life with a sense of achievement and meaning. If you don't feel safe or secure in your life for any reason, this is a big problem that needs to be addressed right away. Not only is it keeping you from being happy, but your safety is on the line. Even if you're safe physically, feeling emotionally unsafe or insecure is ultimately going to keep you from living your life to the fullest.

Just remember to be kind to yourself. Take an hour or two out of each day for self-care, and put effort into connecting with the people you love. You might even find that by helping someone else meet their emotional needs, you can quench your own emotional needs. It's a win for everyone involved!

PROCESSING UNWANTED EMOTIONS

Experiencing unwanted emotions is just a part of being human, but that doesn't make the fact that you're experiencing them any less unpleasant. Learning how to properly process your emotions can be a challenge, but by utilizing the following strategies, you might just find that it's not as hard as you thought it would be. Check it out!

Identify Your Emotions

If you're going to learn how to regulate your emotions, the first thing you'll want to do is identify them. Think to yourself: "what am I feeling right now," and label that feeling with an emotion. When you realize and name the fact that you're experiencing sadness, anxiety, anger, or distrust, it can make these emotions less intense.

Write it Down

It may also be a good idea to write down your emotions and thoughts. Keeping a journal isn't for everyone, but if you have a tendency to overthink things, it's definitely worth a shot. Writing and making art in general is an excellent way to process your thoughts and emotions. You might discover a new passion for yourself!

Talk to Someone

Have you ever talked to a friend or therapist about what you're going through and instantly felt like a weight was lifted off your chest? Even if you just need to vent about work, it's always helpful to have someone to talk to. Talking to a therapist in particular is a great way to process your thoughts and feelings, as therapists are literally professionally-trained to help you do so. You can also gain new perspectives from talking to others about your problems. Your friends and family members may have some surprisingly sound advice.

Practice Mindfulness

Many people swear by doing a mindful meditation exercise, such as a body scan, every morning when you wake up. Being mindful is all about being present. When something is making you anxious, try to focus on your breathing and name what is happening in front of you right there and then. This is an excellent way to ground yourself when you can feel yourself entering the cycle of overthinking.

Engage in Physical Activity

Whether it's running, swimming, or just going for daily walks, you can never go wrong with getting a little bit of exercise each day. It's a good idea to try to get into some sort of exercise routine. Try going for a jog when you wake up in the morning, or join a gym to keep yourself motivated! Exercising is hard at first, but it gets easier and the mental health benefits are absolutely worth it.

How you decide to process your thoughts and emotions is completely up to you. You may go through some trial and error as you find your footing, but you'll find something that works for you! Just be patient with yourself. As with anything else, these things take time and practice.

INTERACTIVE ELEMENT

The only sure way to get better at regulating your emotions is to practice, practice, practice! Here are a few exercises you can do right now to sharpen up your emotion regulation skills:

Make Room For Positive Experiences

Most people tend to focus on their negative experiences rather than their positive ones. This creates a general air of negativity, which can make you feel anxious and unhappy. Using the worksheet below, pick out at least one positive experience you can integrate into each day as a form of self-care. Use the blank spaces to come up with your own positive experiences:

Going for a walk in the woods	Spending time creating something (drawing or writing, for example)	Read a book you've been meaning to read for a while	
Cooking your favorite meal	Do something nice for someone else	Watch your favorite t.v. show	
Spending time with a friend	Take a nice bubble bath	Meditate for half an hour	

Examining and Responding to Your Behaviors

When you feel sad, you typically become withdrawn or quiet. Similarly, when you feel angry, you might find yourself snapping at your friends or coworkers. Using the worksheet below, document your bad feelings and describe the behaviors that typically accompany them. Then, write about an opposite behavior, or a behavior that you'd like to act on instead (i.e. instead of snapping at your coworker, take a deep breath and go for a walk to cool down).

Angry/annoyed		
Sad/upset		
Scared/disgusted/fearful		

SUMMARY BOX

Your thoughts and emotions are beautiful and complicated. Sometimes it feels like they're coming at you all at once! It's important to remember that you don't want to avoid your negative thoughts and emotions. In fact, it's best to acknowledge that they're happening, and that you're feeling a specific type of way. This will keep you grounded and help you feel more in control of your thoughts. The more you practice things like mindfulness and self-care, the easier this will get! Just stick with it.

SEGUE

One of the main concerns people tend to have about breaking free from their overthinking habit is that they could possibly fall back into their old ways. Consider your life and the choices you've made thus far. You've got to be sure that you're overcoming your overthinking tendencies in a way that's actually effective — which is what we'll dive into next.

4

THINK ENOUGH, BUT NOT TOO MUCH

> *"In a moment of decision, the best thing you can do is the right thing to do, the next best thing is the wrong thing, and the worst thing you can do is nothing."*

— THEODORE ROOSEVELT

One of the biggest problems people with overthinking tendencies deal with is indecision. If your thoughts are disorganized, chances are your decision-making skills are going to take a hit. It doesn't help that you have to make a lot of important decisions when you're in your mid-twenties and early thirties, too! This is the age bracket where a lot of people go through things like career changes, health scares, and financial difficulties. It's also pretty common to get married and start having babies around this age, which is obviously a *huge* deal.

Interestingly, this age bracket also tends to be impacted by the most divorces. About 60% of divorces take place when both halves of the couple are between the ages of 25 and 39. One of the main reasons why this is the case probably has to do with the fact that life, when you're that age, can feel turbulent and unsteady. You're either in young adulthood, or you've just exited young adulthood. As much as you might *feel* like an adult (whatever that means), you've still got a lot to learn. You've still got to find your footing.

This, of course, involves making decisions that are likely going to have an impact on you for the rest of your life. This is understandably scary for a lot of young people. You might, for example, feel like you're deeply in love with the person you're dating at the age of 28, but when they propose, you start to feel a pit forming in the bottom of your stomach. You might ask yourself questions like: "do I really want to spend the rest of my life with this person?" and "what if it doesn't work out, and it was all just a big waste of time?"

It's perfectly valid to ask yourself questions like this. Getting married is a really big decision, and you want to be absolutely sure that it's the right decision for you and your partner. That said, decisions like this are a two-way street. Your partner might be all in on the idea of getting married or buying a house together, but you might not be so sure. And that's okay! The important thing is that you talk to your partner about it so that you can figure out a solution together.

Indecision and lack of communication skills oftentimes go hand-in-hand for people who overthink things. A friend of mine recently got into an argument with her husband because she was terrified by the idea of them buying a house together. It wasn't about the house, or her husband, necessarily. It was about the commitment. Not the mention the fact that houses are super expensive.

Instead of communicating her thoughts and feelings to her husband, though, she pretended like everything was fine and dandy, and that she was fully onboard with the plan. When the time came where she actually had to make a decision, however, she completely froze. Her husband wondered, at first, why she didn't seem to want the house anymore. All she had to tell him, though, was this: "I'm not ready."

Deciding that you're not ready to make that kind of decision yet is perfectly valid. In some cases, realizing that you're not ready to take that next step could be the best and most mature decision you end up making in your lifetime. It's a fine line to walk, though. That's what makes decision-making so complicated and nerve wracking. When making big decision, you need to be able to think logically and rationally. If you let too many "what ifs" cloud your judgment, you could potentially miss out on what could be a life-changing opportunity.

The question becomes: how do you know if you're making the right decision? The short answer is *you don't,* and that's okay! Life is all about taking leaps of faith, but if you overthink things too much, you'll just never know what life truly has in store for you. You'll get stuck in an endless state of analysis paralysis, always wondering "what if" but never taking any actual actions to achieve your goals.

Reflection question: Where do I feel "stuck" in my life? (make a list)

Have you ever felt paralyzed by the sheer idea of having to make a decision? You're definitely not alone. Every decision is like a great tree — branching off into hundreds of possibilities. This might be a little bit overwhelming, but just take a deep breath and keep reaching for the next branch. Don't look down and don't think too much about where the next foothold is going to be. Don't worry. You'll find a gnarled knot or a soft spot in the bark to support your weight while you climb.

Try to accept the fact that while climbing the decision tree, you might find yourself temporarily freezing up. This is normal, especially for those who have a fear of heights (in this case, overthinkers). Remember to be confident, and don't fret — for you are not truly stuck. It can sure as heck feel like you're stuck in the moment, though, so let's go over some strategies you can use to unfreeze yourself and keep moving forward when you get overwhelmed.

HOW TO GET UNSTUCK WHEN YOU'RE FEELING OVERWHELMED

There are a lot of things that can cause you to become "stuck," especially when it comes to making decisions that feel big and scary. Many overthinkers get stuck in a rut simply because they're too hard on themselves. Perhaps you've experienced this yourself. Let's say you've more than adequately prepared for an interview for a job you've always wanted, but while driving to the interview, your palms start to get sweaty. That voice in your head says: "Who are you kidding? You'll never get this job. You should turn around now and go home. Save yourself from the inevitable disappointment."

That voice is so mean, isn't it? Not to mention dramatic. When this voice begins to tickle at the back of your mind, it's perfectly okay to tell it to "shut up." It can't control you. It doesn't dictate what you can and can't do. It may seem like it's trying to protect you (i.e. "save yourself from the inevitable disappointment"), but this is not the case. Your inner critic, in a way, is responding to the fear and anxiety you might be feeling about the changes happening in your life. In other words, it's keeping you from living your life to the fullest.

Change is scary! I won't dispute that. All of us are constantly going through changes, big and small, all of the time. The world spins fast, and it can sometimes feel like too much is happening too soon — especially for those with overthinking tendencies. What a lot of people don't realize is, change doesn't just *happen*. It comes from within you. Changing is fundamentally what's going to get you out of your rut. It's just a matter of knowing how to change when you've been stuck for so long. Let's go over some strategies, shall we?

Start Small

One of the reasons people find change scary is that most people thrive on routine. The idea of changing up a routine you've been following for years can be pretty intimidating, but here's the good news: you don't have to change everything all at once. Start by making small changes to your daily routine. For example, if you order takeout or delivery most days, choose one or two days out of the week where you cook your own meals instead. Making small changes like this will help give you the courage you need to start making big changes in your life.

Change Your Perspective

Taking a break from your daily routine once in a while is a great way to eventually break out of it. Introducing things like meditation, regular exercise, and healthy eating into your routine can help you gain new perspectives (as well as make new friends)! Opening your mind to new experiences and different perspectives is one of the most important parts of changing. It can help you gain insight on what's actually possible for your future as well as give you the confidence you need to achieve your goals.

Explore What Your Purpose Is

Feeling like your life has purpose is a crucial emotional need for most people. Take some time to consider what really makes you happy, and what has made you feel fulfilled in the past. Maybe you used to volunteer at an animal shelter, or perhaps you spent one night a week serving dinner at a soup kitchen when you were a teenager trying to beef up your college applications. Consider and reflect upon what made you lose sight of your true purpose in life, and do what you need to do to gain that sense of purpose back.

Believe in Yourself

You've probably heard this one before, but that's just because it's really good advice! People who seem to have it all figured out will usually tell you that life is about 90% confidence. There's quite a bit of truth to this. Forcing yourself to step outside of your comfort zone once in a while can make you feel like you can truly do anything you set your mind to — and you absolutely can! Believing in yourself often requires retraining your brain. The first thing you'll want to do is stop saying things like: "I can't do this" or "I'm not good enough." The fact of the matter is, you really don't know what you can and cannot do until you try.

Let Go of Your Past

Whatever may have happened in the past cannot be undone. If you're constantly ruminating on mistakes you made years ago, you're going to have a hard time being happy in life. Some mistakes — and some trauma — can be especially hard to live with. I completely get it. However, forgiving yourself (and others), and letting go of the mistakes you made in your past is a necessary part of changing for the better and finding happiness. Consider this quote from the hit 2014 television show *Bojack Horseman*: "It takes a long time to realize how truly miserable you are and even longer to see that it doesn't have to be that way. Only after you give up everything can you begin to find a way to be happy."

HOW DO YOU KNOW WHEN YOU HAVE ENOUGH INFORMATION TO MAKE A SMART DECISION?

In this day and age, most people get the majority of their information from the internet. This honestly isn't great, but the internet can actually be helpful if you know where to look. When gathering information to help you make an informed decision about something, it's a good idea to take a few different factors into consideration. You should start by analyzing the possible outcomes of the decision you're trying to make. Some find it helpful to make a list of the various pros and cons!

You should also trust your gut when it comes to the quality of the information you're seeking. If your body is trying to tell you something is off about the information you've gathered, try to seek out other, more credible information from a better source. In general, you'll know whether or not you've gathered enough information to make a decision based on how confident you're feeling about it.

Try to keep in mind, however, that with every decision comes a leap of faith. Gathering information simply makes the gap you have to leap over a bit smaller.

HOW TO MAKE GOOD DECISIONS

Like most adult human beings, you've probably had to make hundreds of decisions throughout your life already. Some of these decisions have been small (i.e. having to decide what you want to eat for dinner), while others have undoubtedly been massive (i.e. "Should I marry this person?" "Should I quit my job?") Making decisions is hard, and you can't always know in the moment whether the decision you're making is a good one.

When making an important decision, you've got to remember not to let your stress influence you too much. It'll be there, for sure, but you don't have to let it send you into a state of analysis paralysis. Just take a deep breath. Everything will be okay. If possible, you should also give yourself some time and space to really think about the decision you're trying to make. Go for a walk, and weigh your options. Try to remain calm so that you can think rationally about this.

It might also be helpful to get another person's perspective on the decision you have to make. Gaining outside perspectives from your friends and family members can help you see your situation in a brand new light. Talking these things out can also help you process your thoughts and feelings, which means you'll be able to make your final decision with a clear head. Remember to trust your gut and take a leap of faith. No matter what you decide, it'll be well worth it in the end.

HOW TO BE AGILE AND RESPONSIVE WHEN LIFE GETS TOUGH

People who overthink things tend to freeze up when life gets exceptionally difficult. This is part of the "fight, flight, or freeze" response system your body uses when you're faced with something that makes you fearful. Learning how to be agile and responsive when dealing with something scary takes a lot of time and effort, but it's definitely worth it. One helpful thing you can do when faced with tough situations is a risk assessment. I'll go over how to do a risk assessment below to make things a bit easier.

HOW TO DO A BASIC RISK ASSESSMENT OR ANALYSIS

1. Identify the Hazards

Each decision you make comes with its own set of potential hazards, and it's important to do your best to identify them. This is mostly a matter of trial and error and gathering necessary information. Before you serve peanut butter cookies to your friend, for example, you should double-check whether or not they have a peanut allergy.

2. Consider Who May Be Harmed and How

It's always a good idea to think about who your decision-making process will impact, both positively and negatively. Let's say, for example, that you're trying to decide whether or not to move out of your parents' house, get married and get an apartment with your partner. While this may hurt your parents' feelings, it's probably going to be the best option for your mental health, your romantic relationship, and your future as a functioning adult.

3. Evaluate and Remove the Risks if Possible

Let's build on the example from above: you're moving out of your parents' house, and this hurts them because it makes them feel as if you don't like living with them or that you don't need them anymore. You might worry that moving out will damage your relationship with your parents, but you shouldn't let this worry keep you from moving out. That will only cause resentment to build. Talk to your parents. Let them share their feelings, and then share your own perspective on the matter. You should eventually be able to find some common ground.

4. Record Your Thoughts

As always, it's a good idea to keep a record of your thoughts and feelings. Writing down what you're feeling about making a certain decision can help clear out any brain fog, meaning you'll be able to make your final decision with a clear mind. This should also help you stay organized. A journal is a great place to make a pros and cons list as well as write out any complicated emotions you might be having about the potential consequences of making your decision.

CONTINGENCY PLANNING

Sometimes, things don't pan out the way you want them to. Perhaps you didn't end up acing that job interview, or maybe you went on a date that ended in disaster. Either way, when making plans and decisions, it's always smart to have some sort of back-up plan in place. Contingency planning can also help you remedy the anxiety that often comes with making decisions. When you have a plan b, you won't have to worry about what might happen if your original plan doesn't work out.

Reflection question: Where is fear keeping you stuck or holding you back in your life?

FEAR-SETTING

While doing my research, I learned about a method called "fear-setting." Employing fear-setting (a method created by Tim Ferriss) into your daily life can help you handle high-stress situations and eliminate analysis paralysis. To put it simply, fear-setting is visualizing all of the bad things that could possibly happen in any given situation, therefore making it possible for you to move forward with making difficult decisions without your fear and anxiety getting in the way.

Fear-setting has a lot to do with stoicism, which is essentially the concept of enduring pain without displaying the fact that said pain is bothering you. Practicing stoicism can basically trick your brain into thinking painful experiences actually *don't* bother you. Mind over matter, you know?

INTERACTIVE ELEMENT

I'd like to give you an opportunity to practice a little bit of fear-setting right now. Using the worksheet below, define the worst things that could possibly happen to you. In the next column, list the ways in which you could potentially stop these bad things from happening. In the last column, list how you will repair each bad thing if it does end up happening.

Define	Prevent	Repair

SUMMARY BOX

Making decisions is never easy, especially for overthinkers. When it feels like your thoughts are all over the place, it can be difficult to make a decision that's based on logic and reason — meaning you may risk making a potentially wrong decision. Thankfully, though, there are plenty of strategies you can use to make decisions more effectively. It's also important to consider the fact that a lot of people who have difficulties making decisions are afraid of change. This fear of change is the reason overthinkers often find themselves stuck in a rut. However, it doesn't have to be this way! By changing up your routine, opening your mind to other perspectives, and employing methods like contingency planning and fear-setting, you can conquer your fears and become a better decision-maker.

SEGUE

Overthinking everything all the time is not just exhausting — it's also incredibly overwhelming. Being overwhelmed can occasionally cause you to act irrationally. You might find yourself snapping at your loved ones or breaking down in the middle of a workday. In the next section of this book, I'll talk about what you can do to reclaim your life when it feels like you're drowning in the overwhelm.

Here's the thing: you can help others by leaving an honest review of this life-changing book. And the best part? It won't cost you a dime.

So let me ask you this: would you help someone you've never met, if it didn't cost you money and you never got credit for it? If so, here's your chance. You can help someone just like you, who's seeking information but unsure where to look. You can be the one to guide them towards this incredible resource.

By leaving a review, you can help:

- One more person conquer their anxiety
- One more person get a good night's sleep
- One more person make confident decisions
- One more person live a life free of negative thoughts

And all it takes is less than 60 seconds of your time.

If you're listening to the audiobook, simply hit the three dots in the top right of your device, click rate & review, then leave a few sentences about the book with a 5-star rating. If you're reading on Kindle or an e-reader, scroll to the bottom of the book, then swipe up and it will automatically prompt a review. And if for some reason the functionality has changed, you can go to the book page on Amazon or wherever you purchased the book and leave a 5-star review there.

By helping others, you're also helping yourself. People who help others (with zero expectation) experience higher levels of fulfillment, live longer, and make more money. So why not make a difference in someone else's life today?

Thank you from the bottom of my heart. Now, back to conquering overthinking!

5

END THE OVERWHELM

> "*Nothing can harm you as much as your own thoughts unguarded.*"
>
> — BUDDHA

For those of us with overthinking tendencies, it's quite easy to want to curl up into a little ball and not talk to anyone for hours on end. Like anyone else, we have our especially bad days. Oftentimes, our thoughts are so intense and plentiful that they tire us out. If you've ever felt overwhelmed and exhausted by your thoughts, just know you're not alone in feeling like this.

By now, you're probably well aware of how emotionally labor-intensive the cycle of overthinking can actually be. Not only is it overwhelming, but it can also be quite isolating. It can make you feel like you're "losing it" in the most invisible sort of way. You're slipping through the cracks, and at times it feels like no one cares or even notices how much pain you're in.

It's quite normal to feel helpless when you get trapped in the cycle of overthinking, but I want you to know that snapping out of it (so to speak) is totally possible. Keep in mind that *you're* the boss of your own thoughts. *You're* the one who's in control here. Are you ready to reclaim your life?

Reflection question: How often do I feel life is too much for me?

You know when you're lying in bed at night, staring at the ceiling and listening to your thoughts get louder and louder in your mind? So much for sleeping. Your brain is wide awake, and it thinks you should be too. Never mind the fact that it's two in the morning and your partner fell asleep the second their head hit their pillow.

All you want to do is sleep, but your thoughts are practically bouncing off the walls. You're deep into the overthinking cycle, needlessly stressing about tomorrow and the next day and the day after that. It almost feels like your brain *has* to have something to stress about, or else it can't function properly. "This is just how I operate," you'll tell yourself and others, half-joking, half-serious. "I'm a perfectionist."

Being a "perfectionist" is all good and well — and hey, it's a great look for job interviews — but (as a perfectionist myself), I've noticed that people with this particular personality trait often overdo it by quite a lot. Perfectionists also tend to be really, really hard on themselves. Let's say, for example, that you work in an office building. You show up to work fifteen minutes early every day with not a single hair out of place. You do your work without error, socialize cordially with your coworkers at lunchtime, and go above and beyond without making a big deal about it.

Any yet… nobody seems to appreciate all that you do. You think to yourself "this company would fall apart without me." When you get home from work, you pour yourself a glass of wine. Your eye starts to twitch. "Imagine if I just didn't show up for work tomorrow?" The thought makes you giddy, but you'll never actually do such a thing. Even if your job makes you miserable, you'll show up in the morning, fifteen minutes early like you always do.

I'm not trying to call anyone out, by the way. It's just that there's something very wrong with this picture, but it can be difficult to see that when you're the one living this kind of life. A friend of mine once told an interviewer that she "thrives in chaos" and she got the job. I found this funny because although "thriving in chaos" is a heavily wanted trait in workers (especially in fast-paced work environments), nobody actually thrives in chaos.

My friend was a high-functioning overwhelmed overthinker, which means she worked herself half to death before realizing she was harming herself more than helping herself. We're humans, not robots! If you robotize yourself, people are going to think they can take advantage of you. If you use your overwhelmed feelings to fuel your own robotization, you're never going to have the time to take a rest and actually address those feelings.

Mental overwhelm, as it turns out, is a bit complicated. Most of us know what it's like to be overwhelmed, but very few of us know how to calm down when we get overwhelmed. Stick around, because that's what we're going to examine next!

WHAT IS MENTAL OVERWHELM?

When a circuit breaker gets overloaded with electricity, it tends to immediately shut down. The system essentially gets overwhelmed because it's trying to handle way too much. Your brain and body works in a very similar way. If you have too much on your plate, or there are too many thoughts bouncing around in your head, you're going to have a difficult time functioning.

Mental overwhelm is an emotional state that you're probably quite familiar with if you're prone to over-thinking. When something feels too challenging — when life starts to feel like all too much — your brain and body go into panic mode. You might feel like your heart is beating too fast or like you're on the verge of tears all of a sudden. You might snap at your coworkers or your significant other, or break down when someone asks you if you're okay.

Being overwhelmed is more than just being stressed out. When you're overwhelmed, you feel like you're being buried alive by your thoughts — which is a terri-fying experience. Because your thoughts are so all over the place, you might find that you have a hard time verbalizing *why*, exactly, you're feeling this way. When someone asks you "what's wrong," you might burst into tears and say: "I don't know!"

Coping with being overwhelmed can be challenging, but it's definitely possible if you have the right tools on hand. Realizing that you're overwhelmed and naming that feeling is a good place to start. When you begin to feel stress building up in your brain and body, take a deep breath and repeat this mantra in your head: *I'm just feeling overwhelmed right now, but it's only temporary. This too shall pass.* If you can, remove yourself from any high-stress situations or environments you might be in. If there's a problem you need to solve, you can enter back into that space when you're ready.

WHY TOO MUCH COMPLEXITY LEADS TO MENTAL BREAKDOWN

The world (and adult life in general) is far more complicated than it used to be. As millennials, we've been through a lot in our short lives — extreme political divide, people's rights getting taken away, a global pandemic, climate change, extreme inflation in conjunction with working wages that frankly aren't livable in this economy — you name it. Our current society is ruled by social media and automation. It's a drastic change, and this change is taking place during our most formative years. Of course we're overwhelmed.

Feeling like the world is in shambles tends to ignite a heavy sense of despair, which most people aren't equipped to deal with. This despair oftentimes turns to anger, and anger eventually dissipates into defeat. And so, you become complacent. You go through the motions, waltzing through this topsy-turvy world on autopilot. When you're in a constant state of over-whelm, it's difficult to know what else you're supposed to do.

I'm here to tell you that you don't have to live like this. There may be a number of reasons life feels too compli-cated for you to properly handle, but there's one reason in particular that a lot of people don't take into consid-eration: you're actually adding to your own overwhelm. Now, this is not your fault. The world *is* complicated, so it's only natural for your life to be complicated as well — especially considering the fact that society is built on capitalism and productivity is valued over everything else.

It might be difficult to pinpoint how exactly you're making your life more complicated than it needs to be, so let's break it down below:

1. You're Constantly Worrying

Worrying drains your energy, so if you're constantly worrying, chances are you're going to feel exhausted most of the time. A lot of people with overthinking tendencies spend more time worrying about the future than they do living in the moment. Let's say, for exam-ple, you're attending your mom's sixtieth birthday party and everyone around you seems to be happy and stress-free. Meanwhile, instead of celebrating with everyone else, you're worrying about the presentation you have to give at work next week. So, you see? Worrying too much is preventing you from actually living your life.

2. You're Trying to Control Everything in Life

Everyone wants to feel like they have some semblance of control in their lives. Many people end up burying their fears in order to avoid facing them, which can provide a temporary illusion of control. However, the truth is, if you feel like you need to control absolutely everything in your life, you're letting your fear control you. The need for control comes from a place of fear, after all. There's a reason our previous president behaved the way he did while in office. Once you learn to accept that you can't control everything, you'll be significantly happier.

3. You're Basing Your Happiness on the Happiness of Others

If you want to find happiness, that happiness has got to come from you. You've undoubtedly seen your friends posting on social media about how gosh dang wonderful their lives are, and perhaps this has made you feel insecure. You might think: "how does this person already have a house and a husband and a baby? I can barely pay rent for my apartment!" What you've got to realize is that the happiness and success of others has nothing to do with your own happiness and success. Comparing yourself to others is only going to make you more dissatisfied. Take a breath, and maybe take a break from social media for a while. This is your life, and you get to decide how you want to live it.

WHAT ARE THE SIGNS THAT A BREAKDOWN IS IMMINENT?

What is a nervous breakdown? Why do nervous breakdowns happen? The term "nervous breakdown" actually has a bit of a negative connotation these days, but it's still widely used by the public to describe what happens when a person loses their ability to function due to a mental health crisis. When you're having a mental health crisis, you might feel like you have a total lack of control. You may find it difficult to function at work as well as do things like eat, sleep, and communicate with others.

Having a mental health crisis is a scary experience, but if you're aware of the signs, you might just be able to stop it from happening. When you're on the edge of a mental health crisis, you'll probably start feeling some symptoms of anxiety — such as nausea, trouble breathing, and cold sweats. You might feel dizzy or like your heart is beating inside of your throat. If you can, sit down and ask someone for a glass of water. Tell yourself: "this too shall pass," and try to focus on your breathing.

Those who are at risk of having a breakdown typically start showing signs days in advance. They might miss social events they had previously claimed they were looking forward to, or they might call out from work multiple days in a row. People in the midst of a mental health crisis tend to isolate themselves and skip out on things like exercising and practicing proper hygiene. Why, you might ask? Because when you're having a breakdown, doing these things feels impossible.

There are a number of things that can cause someone to experience a mental health crisis. When you go through something traumatic, such as a bad breakup or the loss of a loved one, your various systems tend to get overloaded and eventually shut down. Breakdowns like this are unpleasant, but they're treatable. A combination of cognitive behavioral therapy and medication has been proven to be quite beneficial for most.

Reflection question: Can I recognize when I am overwhelmed and create a plan of action to quickly depressurize when it occurs?

Consider what happens when a pressure cooker has too much pressure building up inside of it. Eventually, the stress becomes too much for it to handle and it blows its lid. In order to keep your beans or delicious stew from splattering all over your kitchen, you need to make sure that your pressure cooker is actually able to release pressure.

The question is, when you're overloaded with stress, how should you go about depressurizing yourself? Let's say you have a high-pressure job where people are demanding things of you all day every day. After a certain point, you might feel like you're going to explode. Any person would. Like I mentioned before, we're humans, not robots. When you feel this way, it can be helpful to have some strategies on hand to create immediate ease. This can be achieved by simplifying your life and giving yourself some room to breathe.

If you feel like you have too much on your plate, take a beat and consider this: what can I drop, defer, or delegate? If you have an onslaught of unproductive meetings on your schedule, for example, you should go ahead and drop those. They're time-wasters, anyway, and are only contributing to your stress. Consider which tasks need to be done right now, and which tasks are less urgent. Defer your less urgent tasks until a later date, and focus on what needs to be done in the moment. This will help you stay organized, focused, and calm. You can also delegate important tasks, which essentially means entrusting others around you to complete the tasks you simply don't have time for. Remember: there's nothing wrong with asking for help when you need it!

HOW TO SIMPLIFY YOUR LIFE

Like most human beings, your life is probably chock-full of things to do, places to go, and people to see. It's normal to feel overwhelmed by all of this, especially when more things keep getting added to your already full plate. Contrary to popular belief, it is actually okay to not finish everything that's been placed in front of you. It's really not the end of the world, and everything will be okay. Ask a friend or a coworker to help you eat if it feels like too much to consume on your own. After all, overeating can make you sick.

Simplifying your life is all about removing distractions and unnecessary tasks. It's a big part of taking care of your mental health and practicing self-care. Try to think of your life as a cluttered work desk. If your desk becomes too cluttered, how are you supposed to get any work done? If you're not sure where to start, try making a list of all of the things in your life that feel like clutter. For example, if you have an in-person meeting scheduled with a client that could easily be covered by sending a simple email, cancel the meeting and send the email. Your client will probably appreciate it as well!

One of the most common reasons people feel stressed out is because they're trying to chase too many goals at once. Consider your list of goals, and simplify it. Removing certain goals from your list doesn't mean you'll never achieve them, it just means you don't have to achieve them *right now*. Using fewer words and not engaging with drama can also be quite beneficial when you're trying to simplify your life. You might be tempted to talk with your coworkers about who got the receptionist pregnant, but that's clutter. It's *junk food*. You'll be much happier if you mind your own business. Just do you!

You can also effectively manage your stress by dividing up your various tasks into more manageable chunks. This can be especially helpful for people with mental health issues like generalized anxiety and ADHD. Consider Cinderella: her evil step-mother gives her a long list of things to do every day. She shouldn't have to do all of these ridiculous tasks, but she kind of has to — at least until her prince comes around and has her try on the glass slipper.

I've always found it kind of amazing that Cinderella is able to look at this long list of tasks and just do them, but perhaps she's able to get everything done because she does one task at a time and breaks her work into more manageable parts. When you've got a lot on your plate, don't look at all of the food at once. This will only create more stress. Work on the side dish first, then the salad, *then* the main course. You'll thank yourself for taking it slow, and you should have no problem cleaning your plate in the end.

SUMMARY BOX

Being overwhelmed is an unpleasant feeling, but it's important to keep in mind that it's not a feeling that will last forever. By decluttering and simplifying your life, you can avoid entering the realm of overwhelm, meaning you'll be that much closer to achieving peace and happiness. Remember: you don't have to control everything in your life, and the way others are seemingly living their lives has nothing to do with you. When you feel like you're in danger of having a mental health crisis, sit down, drink some water, and take a deep breath. Remember: *This too shall pass!*

SEGUE

When anxiety kicks in, what should you do? Effectively coping with anxiety takes time and practice, but with the right tools and strategies, you should find that your anxiety is more manageable than you thought it was. In the next section, I'll discuss some strategies you can use to calm down quickly in the event of an upcoming anxiety attack. These strategies have worked well for Lauren and I, and I hope you'll find them helpful as well!

6

FAST CALM

"Worrying does not take away tomorrow's troubles; it takes away today's peace."

— RANDY ARMSTRONG

There's not exactly an end-all, be-all "cure" for overthinking, but there *is* a pretty decent "first aid kit" of sorts you can carry around with you. This first aid kit should help keep you calm when you enter the overthinking cycle and begin to feel overwhelmed. Try to keep in mind that first aid kits come with "fast fixes" for injuries — such as bandages, gauze, cleansing wipes, and antiseptic cream. These things can be incredibly helpful, but if your injury is serious, you should really go to the doctor after dressing your wound.

It's the same with mental health. When your sympathetic nervous system gets triggered by a stressful event, the best thing you can do to calm down is engage your parasympathetic system. I'll discuss how you can do this in a minute, but I just want to stress the importance of seeking help from a mental health professional if you want to do more than just put a bandaid over your emotional cut.

Before we get into the ins and outs of the sympathetic nervous system and the parasympathetic nervous system, let's do a deep dive into something called the "fight-or-flight" response. The fight-or-flight response is a fascinating psychological phenomenon that tends to occur when you're faced with a stressful event or situation.

When I was eight or nine years old, one of the kids in my neighborhood used to ride barefoot on the spokes of my bike. This was obviously a bad idea, but we were just kids. We didn't really take the time to think about what could possibly go wrong. Anyway, one day, I took a spill while my friend was — you guessed it — standing barefoot on my bicycle spokes. His foot got torn open, so much so that the bone was sticking out.

I remember screaming and running to go get my mom. Even at that young age, this wild event triggered my fight-or-flight response. In retrospect, I probably shouldn't have left my friend lying there with his bone out, but I had to get help. It also made me pretty sick to my stomach, seeing his bone sticking out like that. I couldn't help it. It was just how my body responded.

Thankfully, my friend was okay. His parents got him to the hospital as quickly as they could, and he eventually recovered. It just goes to show that it's amazing what the human body is capable of, especially when it comes to healing itself. The same can be said about the human brain. No matter what you've been through — no matter how you responded to certain events in the past — healing is always possible.

There are three basic stages of the fight-or-flight response you should be aware of, namely the alarm stage, the resistance stage, and the exhaustion stage. If you've ever had to bring a friend or loved one to the E.R., or have found yourself in an emergency situation, you're probably well aware of these stages. Just for kicks (and to make things a little easier to understand), let's explore these stages by looking at a potential scenario.

Let's say you're going on a hike with your friends in the woods when all of a sudden you come upon a mountain lion. You're in the middle of nowhere — miles away from your car in the parking lot — and the hungry lioness seems to be stalking you. Each person in your friend group is going to experience either a fight-or-flight response to this event. Some will turn and run, which, just to be clear, is *not* what you should do if you come face-to-face with a mountain lion. Some might try to make themselves large, or throw rocks at the mountain lion to try to get it to go away. These actions illustrate what generally happens during the alarm and resistance stages of a person's fight-or-flight response.

After everything is said and done, you'll enter the exhaustion stage. It's pretty common for people to cry during this stage, as it typically ignites a sense of grief mixed with relief. Perhaps the mountain lion left you and your friends alone, but not before it bit someone on the ankle. You've got to rush that person to the emergency room now, but hey, at least everyone survived.

THE SYMPATHETIC NERVOUS SYSTEM AND THE PARASYMPATHETIC NERVOUS SYSTEM

The fight-or-flight response, as you may have guessed, has to do with the body's sympathetic nervous system. During sudden and stressful events, your body releases hormones that trigger the sympathetic nervous system to have a particular response. The hormones that get released are meant to prepare you to either fight your way out of the situation or run away to protect yourself from harm.

Your body can stay in a state of fight-or-flight for 20 to 60 minutes after the threat has already dissipated. This can be pretty unpleasant, but don't worry. Your parasympathetic nervous system will eventually return to its normal hormonal levels, which means you'll finally be able to calm down. This is why it's recommended to activate your parasympathetic system whenever you find yourself in a situation that's stressing you out.

The thing is, it's pretty rare to find yourself in a situation where it's actually necessary to fight or flee. When your body senses that you're scared or stressed out for any reason, however, it'll begin to enter into that fight-or-flight state. To put it simply, your body often overreacts to stressors that aren't actually that big of a deal. This is where activating your parasympathetic nervous system can really come in handy.

HOW ACTIVATING YOUR PARASYMPATHETIC NERVOUS SYSTEM CAN LOWER STRESS

While the sympathetic nervous system prepares you to deal with stressful events, the parasympathetic system is what helps you de-stress. The question is: how do you go about activating your parasympathetic nervous system? It's not like there's some sort of on-and-off switch for these kinds of things, however, engaging your parasympathetic nervous system is more simple than most people realize.

Needless to say, the world we're living in is a stressful one. Because of this, your fight-or-flight response is essentially on standby. For young women in particular, just walking down the street by yourself at night can be a scary experience. Women have been taught that they need to be in a constant state of alert — and for a good but unfortunate reason. The women in my life, Lauren included, have told me about how they have to hold their keys between their fingers when they walk anywhere alone, which is obviously astonishing. Nobody should have to live in fear like that. Nobody should have to feel like they're constantly in danger.

Being in a constant state of alert can cause one's sympathetic nervous system to go somewhat haywire. Your blood pressure rises, and your heart rate goes up. Your pupils dilate, and your palms begin to sweat. Everyone and everything around you could be a potential threat, and so you must always be prepared to go into fight-or-flight mode. At least, that's what your brain and body is telling you. This is especially true if you're prone to overthinking.

That said, it's not like the dangers aren't there. We've all heard stories about young women getting abducted, assaulted, or worse. This is disproportionately true for women of color, who have to deal with an intricate and especially dangerous subset of misogyny. The fact of the matter is, carrying pepper spray is always a good idea when you're in an unfamiliar environment. This is true regardless of gender, but until men learn to act like civilized human beings, women will always have to be that much more aware of their surroundings.

That said, as a young woman, when you get to where you're going, you should be able to let your guard down a little bit — especially if you're meeting up with your friends or your significant other. Even when you get to a safe environment, however, your fight-or-flight response may continue to act up. This is when it's a good idea to engage your parasympathetic nervous system in order to get yourself to calm down a little bit.

Reflection question: How can I be more mindful of when I am being triggered into fight-or-flight?

HOW TO ENGAGE YOUR PARASYMPATHETIC NERVOUS SYSTEM

Your parasympathetic nervous system is responsible for the "rest and digest" response that takes place in your body after you've endured a particularly stressful event. By participating in activities that lower your heart rate and decrease your blood pressure, you can activate your parasympathetic nervous system all on your own. The next time you're feeling stressed out, try out one of these quick strategies to help yourself calm down. You should start feeling better straight away!

Stick Your Face in Cold Water

This may sound a bit odd, but putting your face into a basin of cold water when you're feeling stressed out can actually trigger a physiological response. This method has actually been scientifically proven to stimulate the parasympathetic nervous system. In short, it distracts your brain and body from the fact you're stressed out, meaning your parasympathetic system will be like "oh, okay, time to calm down now." This is why people often splash cold water on their face when they're stressing about something!

Stay Hydrated

Drinking plenty of water throughout the day is one of the best things you can do for your mind and body. The next time you're feeling anxious, pour yourself a nice glass of ice water and drink it slowly. I recommend sitting outside while you drink, especially if the weather's nice. You can never go wrong with fresh water and fresh air, don't you think?

Spend Time Outside

There's a reason people say things like "I need to take a walk" when they're feeling stressed out. Spending time outside, breathing in the fresh air and communing with nature is a great way to calm yourself down. Not only does being outside activate your parasympathetic nervous system, but it can also help you notice all of the beauty in the world. It can make help you gain a bit of perspective and make you feel like maybe it's not the end of the world after all.

Distract Your Mind

When my wife gets trapped in the overthinking cycle, she often asks me to tell her some jokes. I can't tell you how many times I've frantically googled "jokes" on my phone. I also can't even begin to describe how helpful this has been in a pinch! Things like watching movies, listening to music, and singing can also be great distractions when you're feeling stressed out.

Chant a Mantra

Saying a mantra or two out loud (or in your head) can work wonders. The next time you start to get anxious, try saying one of these mantras:

- "My body deserves time to rest and recharge."
- "When I take deep, conscious breaths, my body relaxes."
- "I won't pressure myself, I'll simply listen to my own body."

Saying and repeating mantras while focusing on your breathing is a form of mindful meditation. By convincing your brain that you are, in fact, calm, you can easily calm yourself down. Keep in mind that you may have to repeat your favorite mantra over and over again. Most of the time it won't start working right away, but within a few minutes, you should start to feel better.

Laugh

Did you know that laughing is super good for your health? This is why getting someone to tell you jokes or watch a funny video can be so helpful when you're feeling stressed out. Laughter has been proven to engage your parasympathetic nervous system, so the next time you're feeling a little bit on edge, try putting on an episode of your favorite comedy show and laugh it up!

Move or Jump Around

Engaging in physical exercise releases your excess adrenaline and increases endorphins (happy hormones) in your body. When you're feeling especially anxious, you might be able to destress by running around the block or doing some jumping jacks. This will get your blood pumping, as well as help you calm down a bit.

Get Some Perspective

I always find it helpful to put things into perspective. When you're feeling anxious about something, your problems can seem huge. Many overthinkers develop a sort of tunnel vision for their problems. They become all that's visible. They become all that matters in that

122 | KIRK TEACHOUT

particular moment! However, if you take a step back and put things into perspective, your problems won't feel so big anymore. Remember: you've overcome worse situations before, and you'll overcome this as well.

Practice Belly Breathing

Belly breathing engages your diaphragm, and is an excellent method to use if you feel like you're having trouble breathing as a result of an anxiety attack. When you breathe normally, your breaths are actually quite shallow — and anxiety can make this even worse. I recommend practicing belly breathing for about 5 to 10 minutes every day. Here's how to do it:

- Lie down on your bed with a pillow underneath both your head and your knees. It's important that you find a comfortable position.
- Place one of your hands on your upper chest, right in the middle. Place your other hand on your stomach, just below your rib cage and right above your diaphragm.
- Slowly breathe in through your nose, drawing in breath towards your stomach. You should feel your stomach pushing upward against your hand while inhaling.

- When you exhale, your abdominal muscles should tighten and your stomach should fall downwards. Let the air out through pursed lips and repeat this process as many times as you need to.

Acu/Pressure

Applying pressure to certain points on your body can help significantly when it comes to reducing stress and anxiety. Here's one easy pressure point exercise you can try right now:

- Sit in a comfortable position. Use pillows to support your neck and back if you need to. It can also be helpful to close your eyes while you do this exercise.
- Gently touch the spot between your eyebrows with your thumb or index finger.
- While taking slow, deep breaths, apply gentle pressure to that spot in a circular motion for 5 to 10 minutes.

Allow Yourself to Cry

Laughing and crying are actually quite similar, so it's no surprise that crying is good for you as well. Crying can be an alleviating, purifying experience for most people. It releases tension and makes you feel better when you're in a state of overwhelm. Some people might tell you that crying is weak, but that couldn't be further from the truth! Crying is perfectly human. You should always cry if that's what you need to do.

Create or Do

Engaging in something you're passionate about is an excellent stress-management technique. Not only does it distract your mind, but it also makes you happy. Creating art or writing is also a great way to process your emotions. If you're not particularly experienced when it comes to creating, don't worry. Just give it your best shot! You might even discover a new passion for yourself.

INTERACTIVE ELEMENT

Here are a couple of quick fixes for you to try out when you're feeling stressed or anxious. Keep in mind that these exercises are just suggestions, and you can tweak them however you see fit.

1. Go outside and write down everything you see that's the color orange. Use this worksheet if you'd like!

(blank lined writing space)

2. Use the box below to draw how you're feeling. Don't be afraid to get creative with it!

(blank drawing box)

SUMMARY BOX

The reason you get anxious and overwhelmed largely has to do with the hormones your body releases during stressful events. Your sympathetic nervous system prepares your body to go into a fight-or-flight response — meaning you'll either fight or flee when you find yourself in a situation that your mind and body perceive as dangerous. Your parasympathetic nervous system is what calms you down when the threat in question dissipates. There are a number of methods you can use to activate your parasympathetic nervous system when you're feeling anxious. Some of the best ways to do so include going outside, taking belly breaths, and submerging your face in cold water.

SEGUE

Why do you often find yourself getting trapped in an overthinking loop? What triggers your state of over-thinking in the first place? These are both excellent questions, and it's what we're going to dive into next, so stick around!

7

TRIGGERS

> *"There is nothing either good or bad but thinking makes it so."*
>
> — WILLIAM SHAKESPEARE

When you're stuck in the overthinking cycle, it can be hard to take a step back and consider what's causing you to overthink so much in the first place. Not knowing what's causing your overthinking is actually contributing to your overthinking, which is why getting a handle on your triggers is so important. Once you gain an understanding of what's triggering your overthinking, you'll have a much easier time controlling — and even preventing — your over-thinking habits.

Consider, for a moment, the situations in your life that are currently causing you stress. Perhaps you work in a fast-paced environment, or your landlord decided to increase the price of rent. Maybe you're going through a breakup, or a family member has fallen ill. You may feel like your life has gotten chaotic for a combination of reasons, and this is causing you to think too much about what you don't have control over. Like a pressure cooker, you're about to boil over. You've gotten overwhelmed by everything life has thrown at you, and you're not sure what to do about it.

A friend of mine (who's admittedly a bit of a perfectionist) went through a particularly rough time last year. The good things in his life — his job, his relationship, and his health — were coming apart at the seams. It made him feel like things were never as stable as he thought they were, and that thought alone terrified him. "It's a disaster," he told me, utterly defeated. "Why is all of this happening?"

He began to lose sleep and developed a binge eating habit because he was so overwhelmed. His binge eating, he told me, was the one thing he had control over. Except, he didn't. It was actually — horrifyingly — out of his control, so much so that he had to attend an inpatient facility. He's thankfully doing much better now, but my point is this: the illusion of control is dangerous, and it can snowball faster than you think. In my friend's case, giving into the illusion of control changed his life in a way that was pretty unpleasant.

I'll discuss the illusion of control and other common overthinking triggers in more detail below. Just knowing about these triggers can drastically improve your ability to stop overthinking everything. If my friend had had this particular tool on hand, he might have been able to rein things in before they got as bad as they did. He might have been able to take a step back and think logically about what he was going through — meaning he could have addressed his stressors in a healthy way.

Due to the fact that your brain is working overtime when you're trapped in the overthinking cycle, it can be difficult to keep your thoughts organized. This, as you may have guessed, can make things feel a lot more overwhelming than they actually are. When you're feeling this way, there are a number of things you can do to let off some steam (as previously discussed). It can be especially helpful to know how to avoid feeling this way in the first place, however, which is why we're going to add a new tool to your tool belt in this chapter: understanding your triggers!

Before we dive in, I do want to reiterate the fact that it's okay to feel overwhelmed sometimes. Life is often overwhelming, and some feelings simply need to be felt. Identifying and understanding your triggers is not about avoiding your emotions. It's just a matter of understanding where your emotions are coming from so that you can more effectively address them.

If your typical reaction to stress is to start overthinking about the things you can't control, then that's rather unproductive, don't you think? Learning how to identify and deal with the things that trigger your unproductive thinking can eventually help you reframe your unhelpful beliefs — which is a key part of overcoming overthinking.

Reflection question: How often am I triggered into overthinking? To what degree is it sabotaging my life?

WHAT TRIGGERS YOUR OVERTHINKING?

Overthinking is a very stressful and personal experience. Everyone's different, which means most people will have different psychological triggers that stem from different past life events. Most overthinkers also have to deal with chemical imbalances, which are caused by disorders like anxiety and depression. What triggers your overthinking mainly depends on you, what you've experienced, and how your brain functions. For most people, their overthinking tendencies are triggered by a combination of things.

Young people often find themselves overthinking about money and the future, which is perfectly understandable. Most 25 to 35-year-olds are only just finding their footing, which can make life feel unstable. This is especially true in today's world, where a global pandemic continues to rage and the cost of living is through the roof. As a result of poor financial literacy, many young people have had to face the fact that they're losing more money than they're making. This is obviously stressful, and it can send one into an overthinking spiral about their future.

Most of the time, a person's unhappiness stems from not being able to achieve their goals due to circumstances outside of their control. This is where overthinking often starts. If you can't afford rent at your apartment because the landlord raised the price, how are you ever going to afford a house one day? If you'll never be able to afford a house, how are you going to raise the big, happy family you've always dreamed of? Are you noticing what big jumps these are? Do you see how overthinking can take you from "I can't afford rent" to "I'll never raise a family" in the blink of an eye?

Obviously, not being able to afford rent in your mid-twenties does not immediately mean you'll never raise a family. That's just not logical, and the two things don't really have anything to do with each other. Also, just as a side note, you can raise a perfectly happy family in an apartment. Overthinkers tend to have such specific plans in mind that they're unable to make room for other possibilities. This kind of tunnel vision can be quite bad for your mental health. It can actually block you from achieving happiness. That's why it's a good idea to learn how to identify when you're experiencing tunnel vision about your future, as well as determine *why* you're having tunnel vision in the first place.

The same goes for overthinking. Overthinking is, in part, what gives most people tunnel vision. When you learn how to stop overthinking about your future (and anything else that stresses you out), you'll be able to loosen up and see things in a brand-new light. Let's go over some of the main psychological reasons you over-think everything below. Again, being aware of these triggers should prove to be a useful tool, so you'll definitely want to keep them in mind!

Childhood Learning

Unsurprisingly, overthinking is oftentimes a habit left over from childhood. This makes sense, considering the fact that overthinking tends to be a trauma response for a lot of people. When you were a kid, things might have been scary or stressful at home, and the only way you knew how to combat that stress was by worrying and overthinking about the situation at hand. For example, when my friend's dad was growing up, his alcoholic stepfather was abusive toward his wife and kids. Because of this, my friend's dad spent much of his childhood walking on eggshells. He would worry obsessively about his mom and younger siblings, and do things like clean up the house before his stepdad got home from work to prevent his mother from getting abused.

Obviously, no kid should have to go through this, but these things do happen. Overthinkers are usually accustomed to having to be the glue that holds everything together, and this takes a toll on most people. My friend's dad is still dealing with the trauma he had to endure from his childhood, despite the fact he leads a pretty good life now. In his own family, he's the glue that holds everything together, and I believe he believes that's his role. After all, that's what he learned when he was little. These things can become deeply ingrained in us, and we can transfer them to our kids as well — though we may not always be aware of it.

Understanding the roots of your overthinking problem is important, but you've also got to gain an understanding of what is triggering your overthinking in the present. Overcoming overthinking is complicated, and facing your present is just as crucial as facing your past in this respect.

The Illusion of Control

I've briefly touched on the illusion of control, and for good reason. This is a massive trigger that can be difficult to recognize for a lot of people. When you feel helpless, it's only natural to want to remedy your helplessness however you can. There's a certain amount of desperation overthinkers go through in an effort to alleviate their helplessness (or the helplessness of those around them). The problem is, this desperation only makes it more difficult to think clearly and rationally during stressful events.

Naturally, when someone we care about is going through a hard time, we want to help them. The feeling of not being able to help someone else can be even worse than the feeling of not being able to help yourself. Overthinking about how you can help someone despite your lack of control over a given situation can *feel* helpful, even if your worrying is actually doing more harm than good. Remember my friend's dad from earlier? Well, his mother, for example, used to fuss over his siblings and him for the smallest reasons, which in turn made things more stressful. He'd worry about the fact that they were causing her stress, which, on top of our other stressors, was a lot to deal with.

The fact that his mother had the illusion of control, however, made her feel like she was helping them. Mothers in particular often feel inclined to "fix" things for other people. They especially want to fix things for their children, which is sweet, but it makes it more difficult for their children to face similar issues later in life. This is part of the reason people with overthinking tendencies struggle with conflict so much. Many young adults never learned how to properly deal with conflict as kids, and so they find themselves trapped in the cycle of overthinking when stressful situations come up.

Perfectionism

It's relatively common for people with overthinking tendencies to be perfectionists. To put it simply, perfectionists thrive on the feeling of being perfect. This can be a trauma response, a symptom of Obsessive Compulsive Disorder, or just another personality trait. Many overthinkers are perfectionists for a number of different reasons. For example, a person may have felt inadequate as a child or teenager, and so they're trying to make up for it as a young adult. Some overthinkers feel like they *need* every aspect of their life to be perfect, or else they won't be able to function properly. If this happens to be the case for you, it might be a good idea to speak to a therapist about it.

The perfectionism trigger can be linked to the illusion of control trigger. Needing things to be perfect in every aspect of your life stems from a need for control. If you've lacked control at any point in your life — as a kid or as a young adult — you're going to be hyper-aware of any semblance of control that's slipping through your fingers in the present and future. For perfectionists, the smallest inconvenience — the tiniest imperfection — can make them feel like everything is spinning out of control.

Honestly, one of the best things you can do for yourself as a perfectionist is to let go of control. This is easier said than done, but it's certainly possible if you have the right tools and information on hand. Letting go of the need to control everything is a big part of overcoming your overthinking tendencies. It might be hard at first, but I promise: you'll be much happier after you let go of the things you can't control.

The Illusion of Certainty

To be human is to be uncertain, and yet, we *despise* being uncertain. People with overthinking tendencies oftentimes deny their uncertainty because it's easier than facing the possibility that something might not turn out the way they want it to. For example, let's say you have an interview coming up for a job you've always wanted. You might tell yourself: "I'm going to get this job," without leaving room for the possibility that you won't. Of course, it's good to be confident and optimistic to an extent. To fully deny the possibility of a bad outcome, though, is a good way to get your hopes up.

Now, if you've spent a lot of time preparing for this job interview, you have a right to be confident. It's basically a matter of finding a healthy balance. You don't want to tell yourself that you'll definitely succeed, but you don't want to convince yourself that you're going to fail, either. Either mindset can send you into the over-thinking cycle when brought to the extreme, which can cause you to lose your focus. Expect the best but prepare for the worst. Stay sharp, and stay balanced, and you'll be okay.

Secondary Gain

The thing about overthinking is it can bring out sympathy and pity from the people around you, which can feel pretty nice. A lot of people with overthinking tendencies will seek out this source of sympathy without even realizing it. This can unfortunately sap people's energy, so it's not a good habit to get into if you can avoid it. The last thing you want is for your friends to think of you as an emotional vampire. The problem is, it can be hard for overthinkers to realize that they're feeding off the sympathy of others. Most fail to recognize that this slight secondary gain could actually be fueling their overthinking.

If you struggle with overthinking, it might be a good idea to examine the relationships in your life. Do you find yourself complaining about your life every time you get together with friends? Do you rope them into your cycle of overthinking? Of course, it's okay to vent about your life sometimes, but you won't be the best company if all you ever do is complain. Please understand that I'm not advocating for toxic positivity or anything like that. It's just that it's important to be mindful of how your overthinking affects the people around you.

Fear of Conflict

People who are afraid of conflict and confrontations are usually really good at avoiding these things. This is especially true for overthinkers, as overthinkers are used to thinking their way out of certain situations (despite the fact that this oftentimes doesn't work very well). The problem is, you can't avoid most conflicts forever. Eventually, that problem at work or with your relationship is going to come to a boiling point and you're going to have to do something about it. Continuing to ignore such a problem is only going to make things worse.

Think about it this way: if your stove is on fire, you're not going to ignore it and hope the fire goes away on its own. You're going to grab your trusty fire extinguisher and put the fire out as fast as you can. You can also call the fire department, which could be equated to asking for help from a friend or a coworker if you feel like you can't deal with a certain conflict on your own. You shouldn't fully rely on other people to put out your fires for you, but it's certainly okay to ask for help if you're feeling overwhelmed.

Overgeneralization

People who overthink everything have oftentimes been praised for their critical thinking skills — by teachers and parents alike. In many cases, thinking excessively has always worked for them. Perhaps you did well on a paper in college because you put a lot of thought into it, or maybe you came up with a solution to a problem at work after thinking about it for hours. Naturally, you'd get praised for this, which would reinforce over-thinking behaviors. For people who've used overthinking as a tool their whole lives, it can be difficult to understand where overthinking actually becomes unhelpful.

Again, this has to do with control. When writing a paper for school or trying to solve a problem at work, you have some semblance of control. Therefore, it makes sense to use your thinking skills to figure things out. If you're waiting to hear back after a job interview, or your family member is sick, however, you won't have much control over the situation. This means overthinking and panicking about these things won't be helpful. It will only make you and those around you feel more stressed out.

ROOT CAUSES OF OVERTHINKING SELF-QUIZ

There are plenty of things that could be triggering your overthinking tendencies. This quiz should help you to gain a better understanding of what your triggers are, as well as help you figure out how to effectively combat these triggers. Using the table below, allocate a percentage to each of the following categories depending on how much you feel each category represents a root cause of your overthinking:

Trigger	Percentage (%)
Stress	
Anxiety	
Unresolved past experiences and childhood learning	
Negative self-talk	
Boredom	
Depression	
The illusion of control	
The illusion of uncertainty	
Perfectionism	
Secondary gain	
Overgeneralization	
Fear of conflict	

HOW DO I RECOGNIZE AND RELEASE MY OVERTHINKING TRIGGERS?

One of the main problems people with overthinking tendencies face is the inability to identify and appropriately cope with their overthinking triggers. It's all good and well to understand that you're probably being triggered by something when you find yourself in the cycle of overthinking, but this understanding won't do you much good if you don't know how to take action and head off your overthinking habit.

Achieving happiness and inner peace takes time and practice, but it's definitely possible if you're willing to put the effort in. By knowing what your triggers are, understanding the various signs that you are being triggered, and taking the correct actions to stop these triggers from getting to you, you can end the cycle of overthinking and learn how to address your stressors in a healthy way. Let's get into it, shall we?

Know Your Triggers

While the most common triggers for overthinking are undoubtedly stress and anxiety, you don't necessarily want to chalk it all up to stress and anxiety and call it a day. By not considering all of the possible options, you're doing yourself a disservice. You might think: "well, stress and anxiety are treatable with medication and Cognitive Behavioral Therapy." This is true, but what if you're dealing with more than stress and anxiety? Moreover, what if your stress and anxiety are actually symptoms of a completely different overthinking trigger?

You shouldn't dive too deeply into "what ifs" as that can amplify the problem, but it is important to know and understand all of your possible triggers so that you can effectively acknowledge and combat them. If you realize that your fear of conflict, for example, is causing you to overthink a certain situation, it's important to recognize that as a specific trigger. That way, you can say: "I'm being triggered by this right now, but I don't have to let it overpower me."

Know the Signs That You Are Being Triggered

Studies show that overthinking can cause you to experience mental health issues as well as physical health issues — such as stomachaches, headaches, and insomnia. These are actually fairly common physical signs of anxiety and stress. If you've ever gotten a tension headache during a stressful situation, that's probably why! When you're stressed out, your body releases cortisol, which can weaken your immune system. This can make you more prone to serious illnesses, so it's important to destress as quickly as you can when you find yourself overthinking.

When you get triggered into overthinking about something, you might start to feel like you're physically hot or like your heart rate is elevated. Your hands might clam up and your thoughts will start racing. You'll feel like the only way to get rid of your racing thoughts is to "think" them out, which means more mental gymnastics. When you notice yourself feeling this way, take a deep breath and ground yourself. Try chanting a mantra or splashing some cold water on your face. Keep in mind that everything is going to be okay, and that overthinking is unproductive.

Take Action to Head Off Your Overthinking Fast

We've already talked a little bit about practicing mindfulness to combat your overthinking tendencies. I'd just like to reiterate how important and helpful being mindful in stressful situations can be, especially if something is triggering you. Learning how to stay present in the moment, rather than stressing out about something you won't be able to control in the future, is honestly the key to maintaining your mental health and happiness.

When you feel like you're about to spiral into the endless overthinking cycle, take a deep breath and take a step back from the situation. If you need to, take a walk around the block or write your thoughts down in a journal. Most of the time, if something feels like the end of the world, it's really not. Try to keep things in perspective, and you won't feel so helpless. Remember: it's all going to be okay.

Reflection question: What else can I choose to do, other than overthinking, that can distract me from the habit?

UNDERSTAND HOW YOUR CORE BELIEFS CAN CAUSE OVERTHINKING

Your core beliefs are essentially what makes you who you are as a person. They inform how you see yourself and the world, and can have a significant impact on your judgment and decision-making skills. Some people — especially younger adults who have lost their way in life — don't know what they believe. A big part of life is figuring that out, but still, a lack of beliefs can make one feel rather unstable.

Some core beliefs can help you find your way. They determine the ways in which you interact with the world, and help you stick to your personal values. This is great, but not all core beliefs are created equal. In fact, most people have a mixture of good and bad core beliefs, and it can be hard to differentiate between them. Because a person's belief system is hardly ever black and white, "good" and "bad" might not be the best descriptors. For this reason, I'll refer to "bad" core beliefs as unhelpful core beliefs from this point forward.

People develop their core beliefs — both helpful and unhelpful — from a variety of sources throughout their lives. Unsurprisingly, nature vs. nurture plays a big role. Oftentimes, you'll learn your first core beliefs from your parents, and as you get older, those beliefs might change. Those who come from unloving homes often have to relearn and redefine their core beliefs once they get the opportunity to move out of their parent's house. This can be a confusing process, and it's often what produces overthinkers.

Changing up your belief system might be a scary thought, but it's possible through Cognitive Behavioral Therapy. This type of therapy focuses specifically on helping people connect their behaviors with their thoughts and feelings. It trains your brain to be able to identify unhelpful thoughts and beliefs you might have about the world, yourself, and those around you. CBT can be extremely beneficial for a person with an overthinking habit, which I'll dive into next.

HOW DO YOU REFRAME AND SHIFT UNHELPFUL CORE BELIEFS?

Let's take a look at a few examples of common core beliefs that could be considered helpful and positive. "I deserve to be loved," for instance, is a helpful core belief, as is something like "people are essentially kind," or "my hard work will eventually pay off." These beliefs are typically born from an optimistic frame of mind, but pessimists can learn to think this way, too. As previously mentioned, it's just a matter of retraining your brain.

A lot of people, especially those with overthinking tendencies, will be more familiar with unhelpful core beliefs like "I don't fit in," and "nobody likes me." These negative beliefs often stem from personal insecurities, which a person can honestly spend their whole lifetime overcoming. Unhelpful core beliefs, like unhelpful or unproductive thoughts, are also a product of fear. Like a turtle's shell, they're meant to protect you from harm. However, more often than not, these types of beliefs prevent you from fully living your life.

So, how do you go about reframing and shifting your unhelpful core beliefs? The process isn't going to be easy, but with patience and hard work, it's entirely possible to reframe your negative thinking. The first step in this process is to acknowledge your unhelpful core beliefs. Try not to think of your unhelpful beliefs as "true." After all, they're usually not based in reality. Simply acknowledge that you have these beliefs, and that they're unhelpful and unhealthy. Realize that these beliefs are holding you back from living your life, and that you have to power to change things for yourself.

If you're having a hard time identifying your core beliefs, I recommend trying Cognitive Behavioral Therapy. A good therapist will be able to help you differentiate between your helpful beliefs from your unhelpful beliefs. They will also likely give you a tool kit, which you can use to reframe your unhelpful core beliefs. You won't know until you try!

INTERACTIVE ELEMENT

I want to give you an opportunity to practice identifying and reframing your unhelpful core beliefs below. Remember: core beliefs are *beliefs*, not facts. Just because you feel a certain way about something, that does not make it the absolute truth. Fill out the worksheets below, and see what you discover about yourself.

Core Beliefs Worksheet 1

Complete the following statements. Rather than spending too long thinking about it, try to write the first thing that comes into your head:

I am _____.

Other people _____.

The world is _____.

In the box below, write about how these statements make you feel. What experiences shaped these beliefs? Is there someone in your life that holds similar views?

Consider this: do these beliefs still serve you? What are some core beliefs that would be more productive and positive? Using the space below, reframe these three beliefs to reflect how you'd prefer to be able to see yourself and the world:

I am _____.

Other people _____.

The world is _____.

Write about how you might interpret or react to a certain situation if you're viewing it through the lens of your new core beliefs:

Core Beliefs Worksheet 2

The exercise below is designed to help you identify your negative or unhelpful core beliefs. Keep in mind that unhelpful core beliefs typically center around worthlessness, unlovability, and helplessness. Tick each box that applies below:

- I am helpless
- I am not lovable
- I am vulnerable
- I am inferior
- I am unworthy
- I am stupid
- I am a burden

SUMMARY BOX

Most of the time when you start overthinking, it's because you've been triggered by something. The most common overthinking triggers include perfectionism, the illusion of control, overgeneralization, fear of conflict, and the illusion of certainty. Determining the root causes of your overthinking tendencies is the first step in overcoming your overthinking. It's important to be able to recognize what is causing your overthinking so that you can put a stop to it before you begin to spiral. Your core beliefs also play a big role in your tendency to overthink things. These beliefs have become ingrained in you because of past experiences, and they can oftentimes be unhelpful. Thankfully, with Cognitive Behavioral Therapy, it's totally possible to reframe your unhelpful core beliefs.

SEGUE

If you've ever broken a bad habit before, you know how challenging it can be. If you're willing to put the time and work in, however, you can eventually shift yourself away from your overthinking habit. In the next chapter, I'll go over how habits are formed and how they can be broken.

8

BREAKING THE HABIT

"*Although difficult, change is always possible. What holds us back from making the changes we desire are our own limiting thoughts and actions.*"

— SATSUKI

Have you ever had a bad habit that you just couldn't seem to break? Perhaps you chewed your fingernails when you were in high school, or maybe you picked your nose as a little kid. We all do it! I'm not here to judge. Most people develop habits like these because they're dealing with anxious or stressful feelings, and their bad habits (chewing their nails, picking their nose, etc.) are somewhat comforting. It's like Linus from *Peanuts* with his security blanket. He carries it around everywhere because it comforts him, despite people telling him he has an unhealthy attachment to it.

Overthinking, as you may have guessed, is a bad habit, too. Although it may bring you some semblance of comfort in times of anxiety, it's ultimately preventing you from living your life to the fullest. Now, considering the fact that Linus uses his security blanket as a catapult, a weapon, a Christmas pageant costume, a Christmas tree skirt, and who knows what else, I'm going to give you a less silly example of a bad habit that's hard to break: smoking cigarettes.

A friend of mine recently stopped smoking cigarettes after being a heavy chain smoker for several years. How did he do this, you might ask? Well, as a matter of fact, he read a book. This book helped him realize that smoking was a security blanket — an *addiction* — and that it wasn't actually doing anything for him. All smoking ever did was empty his wallet and destroy his body. It wasn't helping him. It was harming him. Once you realize that your overthinking habit is harming you, you should have very little trouble breaking it.

Remember: overthinking everything isn't actually doing anything for you. It's not soothing your anxiety. It's not opening up new solutions to your problems. It's just making you miserable. If you're anything like Lauren and me, you've probably used overthinking as a vice for most of your life. You're used to overthinking, and you feel like you do it naturally at this point. The thing is, though, all bad habits can be broken. You just have to want to change.

A lot of people don't think about the fact that overthinking is just another bad habit. It's not something that's talked about very often, which is too bad. If more people thought of overthinking as a bad habit, most would have an easier time breaking the cycle. Admittedly, overthinking is less tangible than other bad habits. It happens entirely inside your brain, whereas biting your fingernails is a tactile experience. It's also much harder to hide a nail-biting habit, meaning people are more likely to scold you for it.

It's also worth noting that habits can be quite complicated, especially when they turn into addictions. Most people with smoking addictions, for example, *know* that smoking is bad for them. The problem is, they simply don't care. Showing them pictures of black lungs isn't going to work because they still feel like they're getting something out of smoking. Most adults don't like to be told what to do either, *especially* addicts.

For this reason, if you want to break your overthinking habit, you've got to tell yourself what to do. You've got to keep in mind that you are the boss of yourself. Your thoughts do not own you, and you do not have to do their bidding. Learning how to question and carefully consider your thoughts takes time and effort, but it's definitely worth it. You're taking control of your life, and that's something to be excited about!

Reflection question: What thoughts do I automatically/habitually think without really questioning them?

HOW ARE THOUGHT HABITS FORMED?

The human brain loves routines, repetition, and patterns. There's a reason people dislike change and enjoy solving puzzles. When we notice a pattern or abide by a comfortable routine, we feel happy because we have a sense of what is coming next. In the previous chapter, I discussed the illusion of uncertainty and how humans hate being uncertain. With routines and patterns, there's an utter lack of uncertainty, and most people take significant comfort in that.

Have you ever asked your parents about the state of the world? Perhaps you've heard them utter something like this in response: "that's just the way things are." I've always found it interesting that older adults never seem to question *why* things are the way they are. I also question why we continue to go along with "the way things are" when the way we're currently doing things doesn't work all that well for people. I suppose it's awfully complicated, but still — "that's just the way things are" is such a non-solution.

It's also entirely based on habitual thinking. People are used to the way things are, so why change them? Why risk being uncomfortable for even a short amount of time? It's hard to change a broken system, so you might as well be complacent. I promise I'm not trying to depress you. I'm just being frank. Hopefully, this example will help you consider the fact that you are in your own world. You have your own system, but that system isn't working right now. Are you going to change it, or are you going to be complacent? The choice is yours.

Habitual thinking is essentially automatic thinking. When you learn and reinforce certain behavioral patterns, these patterns get etched into your neural pathways. You grow accustomed to walking along these pathways, so much so that you inadvertently close yourself off from other opportunities. Instead of taking risks that could potentially change your life for the better, you take the same path you always do and deepen the groove. Consider this excerpt from Robert Frost's insightful poem, "The Road Not Taken":

"I shall be telling this with a sigh
Somewhere ages and ages hence:
Two roads diverged in a wood, and I—
I took the one less traveled by,
And that has made all the difference."

As human beings, we want to know where to go (physically and mentally). We're always looking for the easiest way to get from Point A to Point B — the way that we know by heart. The way we know is safe and certain. Sometimes, though, you just have to take a chance. Changing a certain thought habit is always a leap of faith, but it's often well worth it.

That said, you should keep in mind that it won't be easy. Changing a habit is a lot like changing the way you part your hair. You're going against the grain, and it will be uncomfortable for a while. It's important to remember that that's perfectly normal, and that your discomfort will eventually fade. Let's take a look at how you can start to replace your bad habits, shall we?

TO REPLACE A BAD HABIT, YOU CAN TRY THESE STEPS

Most habits start out as defense mechanisms. They typically stem from things your parents told you in order to keep you safe when you were little. For example, when my friend was growing up, he lived by the sea. His mom always told him: "never turn your back on the ocean," which is fantastic advice because the ocean is unpredictable. Now, as an adult, he never ever turns his back on the ocean when he goes to the beach. Perhaps this is just common sense, but for him, it feels habitual. It's like he can hear his mother's voice in his head, and his inner child abides by her advice.

That's an example of a healthy habit, but, like anyone else, I have my fair share of unhealthy habits as well. For instance, I dig my fingernails into my palms and clench my teeth when I'm feeling stressed out. Most of the time, I won't even notice I'm doing this. I'll look down at my hands after the moment has passed and see all of the little crescent-moon indentations in my skin and have headaches from clenching. I've been doing this since I was a kid, and the fact that I do it subconsciously makes it difficult to stop.

Perhaps you have the same or a similar habit, so let's use it as our unhealthy habit example. Now, if we're going to eventually change this bad habit (i.e. replace it with a healthy one), there are a few things we'll need to do. Keep in mind that the following steps can also be applied to changing an overthinking habit.

Step One: Identify Your Triggers

Consider what triggers you to perform your habitual rituals (i.e. overthinking, digging your fingernails into your palms, clenching your teeth, etc). Perhaps there's someone at work who just grinds your gears, or maybe being around too many people on public transportation is too overwhelming. Whatever your triggers are, recognizing and naming them can help significantly. You'll begin to associate your bad habits with your triggers, meaning you'll be more likely to notice yourself feeling compelled to perform a habitual ritual.

Step Two: Find a Replacement Habit

Now that you're aware of your various triggers, you should have some control over the bad habit you're trying to change. Name your bad habit so that it's fresh in your mind. Say to yourself: "I typically react to stress by digging my fingernails into my palms, but I'm trying to stop doing that because it's unhealthy." Consider what you can do instead of digging your fingernails into your palms. Perhaps you can practice belly breathing when you're feeling nervous.

Step Three: Plan and Prepare

If you're going to change your habitual behaviors for the better, you're going to need to come up with a solid plan. Most habits become habits because we inadvertently attach some sort of reward to our habitual behaviors. For example, when you dig your fingernails into your palms, you feel a sense of relief and release. Similarly, when you overthink something, you might feel better because you're tricking yourself into thinking you're being proactive and productive (when you're actually not).

When replacing a bad habit with a healthy habit, it's important to keep this reward system in mind. Once you've figured out a healthy habit to replace your unhealthy habit with, you can decide how this particular habit will be rewarding for you. For example, you'll get the same release from belly breathing that you do from digging your fingernails into your palms. It's just a matter of rewiring your brain!

Step Four: Create Accountability

One of the best things you can do for yourself when trying to kick an unhealthy habit is to ask for help. Find a friend or family member who's willing to be a support system for you, or join a support group for overthinkers! I also recommend creating even more accountability for yourself by tracking your progress in a journal. Writing down your thoughts and feelings each day will help you stay organized as well as aid you in processing what you're going through.

Step Five: Reward Yourself

Changing or replacing an unhealthy habit is hard work! Once you've succeeded in sticking to your new, healthy habit for an extended period of time, you should definitely reward yourself. This can also create a good incentive for you to stick to your good habits. For example, you can tell yourself that you get to order pizza at the end of the week if you continue to follow your new habit. Of course, you shouldn't let pizza as a reward become a *new* unhealthy habit. Moderation is key when it comes to rewards.

Step Six: Be Patient and Persistent

Change doesn't happen right away. I've seen way too many people get frustrated because they weren't able to kick their bad habits within a few days of attempting to do so. You've got to keep in mind that replacing your bad habits with healthy habits is going to take a considerable amount of grit and determination. It's also important to accept the fact that setbacks happen. Your habits are deeply ingrained, and you'll probably find yourself slipping up once or twice in times of stress. Don't give up! Have compassion for yourself and reflect on how you can do better next time.

PRACTICING SELF-COMPASSION

When you're in the process of changing an unhealthy habit, it's important to practice self-compassion. When others are going through something difficult, you typically show them empathy and compassion for their struggles, right? Perhaps you even take care of them for a short time if you love them very much. Well, it's important to show yourself that love and care as well! Overthinkers are highly sensitive and are oftentimes too hard on themselves. Perhaps this is something you've noticed about yourself in the past.

In Chapter 2, we did a deep dive into faulty cognition, which is essentially the concept of experiencing thoughts and feelings that aren't true. It's incredibly common for overthinkers to imagine problems where there really are none. For example, someone with an overthinking habit might feel like their friends are talking about them behind their back when that's actually not what's going on at all. Overthinkers may experience faulty cognition for several reasons, including trauma and past life events.

Those who have issues with faulty cognition tend to inadvertently create unhealthy coping mechanisms, such as avoiding other people or even lashing out at their loved ones. Most overthinkers are somewhat blinded by their faulty cognition, so it's hard for them to see that their coping mechanisms may be harmful to those around them. It also may be difficult for a highly sensitive overthinker to acknowledge that some of their coping mechanisms are unhealthy.

How to Practice Self-Compassion

When you feel like you're overthinking something (i.e. experiencing a faulty cognitive bias), take a deep breath and consider this: you're not a mind reader. Let's say, for example, you feel like your two best friends are talking smack about you behind your back. Ask yourself why you feel this way. What exactly is triggering this thought process? If you really can't get it off your mind, ask your friends if they actually have been talking about you behind your back. Yes, there's always the possibility that they won't tell the truth, but if that's the case, they're not really your friends.

It's also important to keep in mind that everyone is going through their own stuff. Most of the time, the people around you aren't paying you any mind because they're too busy worrying about what other people are thinking or saying about them. Every single person in the world is living a life that is as complex and intricate as your own. Keep things in perspective and focus on yourself. I promise, you'll be just fine.

Like most things, having compassion for yourself takes time and plenty of practice. In part, practicing self-compassion involves reframing your negative core beliefs, which we touched on in Chapter 7. Learning about and practicing mindfulness can also make it easier for you to have compassion for yourself. Those who regularly practice self-love and self-care weren't born knowing how to do that. Through meditation and mindfulness, though, they figured out how to have self-compassion and live happier lives — and you can too!

HOW MINDFULNESS CAN HELP YOU MASTER YOUR MIND, BODY, AND LIFE

There's nothing worse than feeling like you don't have control over your own mind. This lack of control is what makes being an overthinker scary at times. Nobody enjoys feeling like their thoughts are spiraling out of control! That's why learning how to gain control over your mind is so important. When you have a clear and confident mindset, you can tackle anything life throws at you. How does one develop a clear and confident mindset? A combination of strategies could work wonders, but the number one thing that is sure to improve your mindset is regularly practicing mindfulness.

Being mindful essentially involves staying calm, grounded, and clear-headed in stressful situations. You've got to realize that panicking during a stressful life event will only make matters worse. When you allow yourself to be mindful, you're basically accepting the fact that certain things are out of your control. Once you let go of control, you'll have a much easier time handling situations that typically trigger you into overthinking. It's a matter of telling yourself: "This is out of my control right now, and that's okay. This is not the end of the world." Again, it's all about keeping things in perspective!

Now, I'm not saying you have to become a "zen master," but setting aside just fifteen minutes a day to practice mindfulness could make all the difference in your life. When you learn how to utilize mindfulness at work, home, and in other areas of your life, you might just find that the things you typically spend time and energy overthinking about never actually mattered that much in the first place.

Practicing mindfulness gives you a sense of your true wants and needs, meaning it'll allow you to effectively set boundaries with people who stress you out. Being mindful is also a key part of overcoming the various obstacles in your life. You'll be able to think about your problems — and the potential solutions to your problems — in a way that's actually constructive and productive. No more unhelpful thoughts or faulty cognitive biases throwing you off your game!

WHAT CAN HELP YOU BE MORE MINDFUL?

For most people, being mindful doesn't come naturally. This is perfectly okay, and it's the main reason mindfulness is something you should practice regularly. There are a number of ways you can practice mindfulness throughout your daily life, including meditating, focusing on the present moment, reflecting on what's happening in your life, and eliminating multitasking when life becomes too overwhelming. Let's go over these mindfulness methods in a bit more detail below:

Meditation

Contrary to popular belief, the point of meditation is not to become entirely undistracted and free of thought. You're not trying to reach some sort of destination when you meditate. You're simply exploring your mind and making yourself aware of every beautiful moment. Meditating is essentially the opposite of overthinking. Instead of overanalyzing your thoughts, you simply let them wash over you. Instead of letting your emotions get the best of you, you acknowledge and move past the emotions that you'd usually find upsetting. When you practice mindful meditation, you're asking yourself to suspend your judgments for a few minutes. You're allowing yourself to be curious about your mind, rather than being afraid of it. It takes practice, of course, but meditating frequently can truly work wonders!

Reflection

Taking the time to reflect on your past and current life experiences is an excellent way to practice mindfulness. I'm not sure how many times I've recommended recording your thoughts and feelings in a journal throughout this book, but I suppose I can't recommend it enough! When you keep your thoughts and feelings bottled up inside, you risk propelling yourself into the vicious overthinking cycle. Write down your thoughts every now and then, and they won't seem so big and scary. Like meditating, learning how to properly reflect on your thoughts and emotions takes time and practice. Once you get the hang of it, though, you'll find that it's completely worth it.

Focus on the Present Moment

When you start stressing about your past or future, try bringing your focus back to the present moment. Remember: you can't change what happened in your past, nor can you control what's going to happen in your future. The present is what it's all about, and it's worth paying attention to. If you find yourself getting pulled into the overthinking cycle, use your five senses to form connections with what's happening around you. This will help you stay grounded and focused on what really matters.

Stop Multitasking

If you work a high-stress job, you're probably used to multitasking. Or, at the very least, you're used to your boss praising your coworkers for multitasking at the expense of their mental health. The fact of the matter is, the human brain isn't well-designed for multitasking. You might have noticed that your computer has a hard time functioning properly when you have multiple tabs open at the same time. Your brain works in a very similar way. When you take on too much, it gets over-loaded and chaos ensues. Although productivity is valued in our society, you won't be doing yourself any favors by attempting to multitask. Take things slowly, and you'll find that life will be more rewarding (and much more forgiving).

INTERACTIVE ELEMENT

Now that you've learned about mindfulness and how to apply mindfulness to your everyday life, perhaps you'd like to practice a bit. Feel free to participate in the mindfulness exercises I've included below whenever you have the time to do so. If you're feeling confident and clear-headed, why not try the first exercise right now?

Mindfulness Exercise 1: The Raisin Exercise

This exercise will work with any type of food, but I recommend using something small, tactile, and textured — such as a raisin. Hold the raisin in your hand, and pretend as if you've never seen a raisin before. This might feel a bit silly at first, but just bear with me! While holding the raisin, record what you notice about it. You can write in the spaces I've provided below if you wish to:

How does the raisin look? (don't just say "like a raisin.")

_____.

How does the raisin feel? _____.

How does your skin respond when you manipulate it?

_____.

How does it smell? _____.

How does it taste? _____.

This exercise should help you stay grounded and focused on the present. Pretty interesting, don't you think?

Mindfulness Exercise 2: Mindful Seeing

This exercise requires a window with some kind of view. You can also step out into your back or front yard if you want to get some fresh air. Once you're comfortable, look at everything in your line of sight. What do you see? What do you notice? Don't just say "a squirrel" or "a garbage can." Consider the shapes, patterns, and colors of the objects around you. Pay attention to the wind, and how it makes the fallen leaves dance. Observe without being critical. Be aware of your surroundings, and just breathe. Do this until you feel more grounded and connected with the world around you.

SUMMARY BOX

With a little time and effort, you'll find that breaking your overthinking habit is absolutely possible. Most of us are familiar with the feeling of getting trapped in a cycle, but here's what most people don't realize: you're not actually trapped! You have the power to take back your life. By practicing mindfulness and self-compassion, you can keep yourself from falling back into your old overthinking ways.

CONCLUSION

> *"You only have control over three things in your life, the thoughts you think, the images you visualize, and the actions you take."*
>
> — JACK CANFIELD

Overthinking is a surprisingly common problem. People all over the world are plagued by overthinking tendencies, so it's a little bizarre that this particular issue isn't talked about more outside of the mental health and mindfulness communities. To make matters more difficult, people who aren't plagued by overthinking tend to misunderstand overthinkers. If you've ever been called "dramatic" because of your overthinking habit, you know exactly what I'm talking about.

It's important to recognize that nobody is born an overthinker. Like Lauren and me, you likely developed your overthinking habit due to past trauma and undiagnosed or poorly-treated anxiety. The good news is, your overthinking habit is entirely manageable if you have the right tools on hand. Throughout this book, I've provided tools and information that you can arm yourself with when the going gets tough. You've got the power in your hands, and I believe that you can do this.

Pat yourself on the back, and consider all that you've learned throughout this process. First and foremost, understanding your overthinking habit is a crucial step in eventually overcoming it. You've also got to take your faulty cognitive biases into consideration, as these biases tend to be a common cause of overthinking for most people. Understanding your emotions and developing strategies for getting yourself "unstuck" when you feel overwhelmed is also essential.

Furthermore, if you want to overcome your overthinking habit, you're going to need to simplify your life. Oftentimes, we feel overwhelmed because we're trying to take on too much at one time. Sometimes, you can't avoid feeling overwhelmed, but you can remedy it. It's important to listen to your body and use one of the exercises listed in Chapter 6 to help yourself unwind when life feels too stressful. It's also a good idea to identify your triggers and learn how to diffuse your anxiety when you get triggered by something.

Lastly, practicing self-compassion and coming up with a plan to replace your overthinking habit is the key to overcoming it. Try to approach life with more mindfulness, and you'll find your happiness. It's right there, within your reach.

Now, to wrap things up, I'd like to share a success story with you: the story of a recovering overthinker named Claire Seeber. Claire, like many of us, spent way too much of her life worrying about what other people thought of her. She desperately wanted to feel like she was doing well in life — like she was successfully keeping her head above the surface — but this proved to be difficult because she was constantly overthinking everything.

Claire eventually realized that the time and energy she spent overthinking was actually preventing her from living her life. She started questioning her unhelpful thoughts. She asked herself: "why am I thinking about this, and is it worth investing this must energy?" She considered whether a particular worry would even be a blip on her radar in six months' time. She wondered:

"what evidence do I have that this person actually has the opinion of me that I think they do?"

Claire accepted that overthinking was just a part of herself (as it is a part of all of us), but she understood that she had the power to control it. Her story shows that you don't have to be afraid of your overthinking habit. You simply have to ask yourself grounding questions, and rein it in a bit when you feel yourself starting to spiral. Claire is a self-declared "recovering over-thinker," which is a wonderful way to put it. By being more mindful and taking the time to understand her overthinking habit, she eventually changed her life for the better — and you can too!

It's important to keep in mind that there's no "cure" for overthinking. As Claire states in her story, overthinking is simply a part of yourself. When you learn to accept and understand that part of yourself, you'll have a much easier time controlling it. You'll get to live the life you want to live on your own terms without worrying so much about everything. I hope you've enjoyed reading this book as much as I've enjoyed writing it. It would mean the world to me if you left a review, as that will further help people like you who are struggling with overthinking.

Congratulations on finishing "Overcoming Overthinking!"

You've taken the first step towards a life free from anxiety, sleeplessness, indecision, and negative thoughts.

But before you close the book, I have a final request. Would you take a moment to leave an honest review of this book and its contents? Your review can help someone just like you who's seeking information but unsure where to look. It can be the difference between them continuing to suffer or finally finding the help they need.

In the middle of this book, we talked about the importance of helping others. And now, by leaving a review, you have the opportunity to do just that. Again, you can help:

- One more person conquer their anxiety
- One more person get a good night's sleep
- One more person make confident decisions
- One more person live a life free of negative thoughts

By helping others, you're also helping yourself. People who help others (with zero expectation) experience higher levels of fulfillment, live longer, and make more money.

So let's make a difference together. If you're on Audible, hit the three dots in the top right of your device, click rate & review, then leave a few sentences about the book with a 5-star rating. If you're reading on Kindle or an e-reader, scroll to the bottom of the book, then swipe up and it will automatically prompt a review. And if for some reason the functionality has changed, you can go to the book page on Amazon or wherever you purchased the book and leave a review there.

Thank you for taking the time to help others, and in turn, help yourself. You have the power to change someone's life with just a few words. Let's make it happen.

RESOURCES

15 ways to improve your focus and concentration skills. 15 Ways to Improve Your Focus and Concentration Skills. (n.d.). Retrieved March 9, 2023, from https://www.betterup.com/blog/15-ways-to-improve-your-focus-and-concentration-skills

Amy Morin, L. C. S. W. (2023, February 14). *Are you overthinking? here's how to tell.* Verywell Mind. Retrieved March 9, 2023, from https://www.verywellmind.com/how-to-know-when-youre-overthinking-5077069

Anna Katharina Schaffner, P. D. (2023, March 3). *Core beliefs: 12 worksheets to challenge negative beliefs.* PositivePsychology.com. Retrieved March 9, 2023, from https://positivepsychology.com/core-beliefs-worksheets

Barker, W. (2020, February 26). *The 9 emotional needs everyone has + how to meet them.* mindbodygreen. Retrieved March 9, 2023, from https://www.mindbodygreen.com/articles/9-emotional-needs-according-to-maslow-s-hierarchy

Becker, J. (2022, August 22). *The 10 most important things to simplify in your life.* Becoming Minimalist. Retrieved March 9, 2023, from https://www.becomingminimalist.com/the-10-most-important-things-to-simplify-in-your-life/

Buggy, P. (2020, May 19). *Fear setting: The step-by-step exercise Tim Ferriss uses to Conquer Fear.* Mindful Ambition. Retrieved March 9, 2023, from https://mindfulambition.net/fear-setting-tim-ferriss/

Changing habits. Learning Center. (2022, June 6). Retrieved March 9, 2023, from https://learningcenter.unc.edu/tips-and-tools/changing-habits/

Cherry, K. (2022, November 6). *Types of cognitive biases that distort how you think.* Verywell Mind. Retrieved March 9, 2023, from https://www.verywellmind.com/cognitive-biases-distort-thinking-2794763

Cherry, K. (2022, November 7). *The fight-or-flight response prepares your body to take action*. Verywell Mind. Retrieved March 9, 2023, from https://www.verywellmind.com/what-is-the-fight-or-flight-response-2795194

Cherry, K. (n.d.). *Emotions and types of emotional responses*. Verywell Mind. Retrieved March 9, 2023, from https://www.verywellmind.com/what-are-emotions-2795178

Choksi, D. (2021, August 8). *Science explains overthinking*. Medium. Retrieved March 9, 2023, from https://medium.com/indian-thoughts/science-explains-overthinking-b709d0ec4dca

Council, F. C. (2022, October 12). *Council post: 13 ways to overcome negative thought patterns*. Forbes. Retrieved March 9, 2023, from https://www.forbes.com/sites/forbescoachescouncil/2016/05/09/13-coaches-explain-how-to-overcome-negative-thought-patterns/

Edberg, H. (2022, June 10). *34 quotes to help you to stop overthinking (+ my 5 favorite tips)*. The Positivity Blog. Retrieved March 9, 2023, from https://www.positivityblog.com/overthinking-quotes/

Eklof, K. (2020, June 18). *What happens to your body when you overthink?* Edexec. Retrieved March 9, 2023, from https://edexec.co.uk/what-happens-to-your-body-when-you-overthink/

Entefy. (2022, March 31). *How much information do you need to make smart decisions? - entefy: AI & Automation*. Entefy. Retrieved March 9, 2023, from https://www.entefy.com/blog/how-much-information-do-you-need-to-make-smart-decisions/

The Five steps to risk assessment explained. Risk Assessor :: The five steps to risk assessment explained. (n.d.). Retrieved March 9, 2023, from https://www.riskassessor.net/news/detail/five-steps-to-risk-assessment

Garrett, L., Pratt, M., Hasenkamp, W., Goh, C., PhD, B. G. B., Kira M. Newman and Janet Ho, Newman, K. M., & Staff, M. (2023, January 6). *Getting started with mindfulness*. Mindful. Retrieved March 9, 2023, from https://www.mindful.org/meditation/mindfulness-getting-started/

Hanh, T. N. (2022, November 9). *Five steps to mindfulness*. Mindful.

Retrieved March 9, 2023, from https://www.mindful.org/five-steps-to-mindfulness/

How the parasympathetic nervous system can lower stress. Hospital for Special Surgery. (n.d.). Retrieved March 9, 2023, from https://www.hss.edu/article_parasympathetic-nervous-system.asp

How to deal with feeling emotionally overwhelmed - talkspace. Mental Health Conditions. (2022, November 28). Retrieved March 9, 2023, from https://www.talkspace.com/mental-health/conditions/articles/feeling-overwhelmed/

Itani, O. (2022, December 27). *You are what you think: How your thoughts create your reality.* OMAR ITANI. Retrieved March 9, 2023, from https://www.omaritani.com/blog/what-you-think

Kinoshita T;Nagata S;Baba R;Kohmoto T;Iwagaki S; (n.d.). *Cold-water face immersion per se elicits cardiac parasympathetic activity.* Circulation journal : official journal of the Japanese Circulation Society. Retrieved March 9, 2023, from https://pubmed.ncbi.nlm.nih.gov/16723802/

Leo Newhouse, L. I. C. S. W. (2021, March 1). *Is crying good for you?* Harvard Health. Retrieved March 9, 2023, from https://www.health.harvard.edu/blog/is-crying-good-for-you-2021030122020#:

Maughan, T. (2020, November 30). *The modern world has finally become too complex for any of us to understand.* Medium. Retrieved March 9, 2023, from https://onezero.medium.com/the-modern-world-has-finally-become-too-complex-for-any-of-us-to-understand-1a0b46fbc292

MediLexicon International. (n.d.). *Core beliefs: Definition, how to identify, and more.* Medical News Today. Retrieved March 9, 2023, from https://www.medicalnewstoday.com/articles/core-beliefs

MediLexicon International. (n.d.). *What is diaphragmatic breathing? benefits and how-to.* Medical News Today. Retrieved March 9, 2023, from https://www.medicalnewstoday.com/articles/diaphragmatic-breathing

Moderndayomblog. (2021, August 19). *7 signs you're overthinking something as an HSP.* Sensitive Refuge. Retrieved March 9, 2023, from https://highlysensitiverefuge.com/7-signs-youre-overthinking-something-as-an-hsp/

MSW, W. by: I. W., & MD, R. by: K. F. (n.d.). *How to overcome your inner critic.* Choosing Therapy. Retrieved March 9, 2023, from https://www.choosingtherapy.com/overcome-inner-critic/

Raypole, C. (2020, April 28). *How to control your emotions: 11 strategies to try.* Healthline. Retrieved March 9, 2023, from https://www.health line.com/health/how-to-control-your-emotions

schneik4. (2022, December 9). *Overthinking disorder: Is it a mental illness?* Cleveland Clinic. Retrieved March 9, 2023, from https://health. clevelandclinic.org/is-overthinking-a-mental-illness/

Seeber, C. (2022, April 12). *Confessions of a recovering Overthinker.* Circle In. Retrieved March 9, 2023, from https://circlein.com/confes sions-of-a-recovering-overthinker/

Seladi-Schulman, J. (2018, July 24). *What part of the brain controls emotions? fear, happiness, anger, Love.* Healthline. Retrieved March 9, 2023, from https://www.healthline.com/health/what-part-of-the-brain-controls-emotions

Sussex Publishers. (n.d.). *7 ways to get yourself unstuck.* Psychology Today. Retrieved March 9, 2023, from https://www.psychologyto day.com/za/blog/women-s-mental-health-matters/201612/7-ways-get-yourself-unstuck

Thinking too much; and thinking too little. The School Of Life. (n.d.). Retrieved March 9, 2023, from https://www.theschooloflife.com/article/thinking-too-much-and-thinking-too-little/

Visé, D. de. (2022, December 26). *More adult children are living with their parents. parents are not pleased.* The Hill. Retrieved March 9, 2023, from https://thehill.com/policy/finance/3777185-more-adult-chil dren-are-living-with-their-parents-parents-are-not-pleased/

Walker, T. (n.d.). *14 mantras to repeat when things feel stressful.* Shine. Retrieved March 9, 2023, from https://advice.theshineapp.com/arti cles/mantras-to-repeat-when-things-feel-stressful/

What is overthinking disorder? BetterHelp. (n.d.). Retrieved March 9, 2023, from https://www.betterhelp.com/advice/personality-disor ders/what-is-overthinking-disorder/

Wignall, N. (2021, February 17). *7 psychological reasons you overthink everything*. Nick Wignall. Retrieved March 9, 2023, from https://nickwignall.com/7-psychological-reasons-you-overthink-everything/

Printed in Great Britain
by Amazon

32590467R00106